THE PULP

VS.

THE THRONE

ARTIFICE BOOKS

Published by Artifice Books, an imprint of
Curbside Splendor Publishing, Inc.,
Chicago, Illinois in 2015.

First Edition
Copyright © 2015 by Carrie Lorig
Library of Congress Control Number: 2015943118

ISBN 978-1-940430-52-2

Edited by Peter Jurmu
Cover designed by Evan Scott Bryson

Manufactured in the United States of America.

for a pony named Kenneth / for N

THE PULP

VS.

THE THRONE

CARRIE

LORIG

MUCH AFFECTION
FROM THE BOLD
PART / OF THE
RIVER / IT'S A
CRISIS / OF
MOVEMENT

These decibels
Are a kind of flagellation, an entity of sound
Into which being enters, and is apart

— *John Ashbery*

I. THE PULP VS. THE THRONE

y e s mouth-open-certain-mercy-plugs

y e s a-cliff-thrive

y e s a-release-of-near-air

I have been thinking about you I have been passed by weather drowning a socket a clearing I have been c i r c u l a t i n g a socket a clearing I have been Softly Crossed Matter I have been feeding dryer sheets to a heart I have lifted it by my pleasure It swarms in f o s s i l s n o w It drifts in god paper I feel s l u t m o n e y I feel warm I have been thinking about writing to you in this way

This body cavity, this carved in waste, I call the The Pulp Vs. The Throne.

The Pulp Vs. The Throne steals inverted flowers—their late charges and their hard cases
    torn into
THE FALLS, THE FALLS.
The Pulp Vs. The Throne exposes a mass bouquet
aware
   of radar and
         understanding
              touching
                 quietly
                    the floor.
The Pulp Vs. The Throne canopies trick riders into grated plums.
The Pulp Vs. The Throne canopies trick riders into sentence evacuees.
The Pulp Vs. The Throne canopies trick riders into runt garlands.
The Pulp Vs. The Throne is a flare skeleton
                          is a redbutter is
          a grave of lightdye.
The Pulp Vs. The Throne means to be harsh there.
The Pulp Vs. The Throne   is an Activity and a Markway
                        and a Pit of Acknowledgement.
The Pulp Vs. The Throne   is a Sun Cut in Two and the White Sap
                        and a Rough Decimal Caught in it.
The Pulp Vs. The Throne because I never feel safe.
The Pulp Vs. The Throne means to be sweet there.
The Pulp Vs. The Throne pulls threshold fumes into the crookarm of my boom / my boob.
The Pulp Vs. The Throne pulls flinchbelieving into my riveted body.
The Pulp Vs. The Throne pulls veilscalp into my riveted body.
The Pulp Vs. The Throne pulls and The Geography of Needles turns around throated and sold.
The Pulp Vs. The Throne pulls the crookarm of my boom / my boob   It is so bright
attractive   /   insidious   It feels like a square of moonbit   in the sea
                                     I pick up and call RAINLIGHT.

The Pulp Vs. The Throne hears folds

or Undertow Folds or undertow it has
the Tarp Roses in my nervous   I'm so mine
in my nervous / in slash life I expand to uncover
like it's Almond
like it Burns Middles   to have them.

The Pulp Vs. The Throne   SILKY BOLTS FOLLOWED AROUND
ONLY MY LOVE CAN KNOW AND
ONLY BY CUTTING ITSELF WILL IT.

The Pulp Vs. The Throne says, Is this the dirty balcony limb?
The Pulp Vs. The Throne says, Is this the estuary?
The Pulp Vs. The Throne says, Is this the estuary full of WINDOW DRESSING?
The Pulp Vs. The Throne says, Because it's THICK.
The Pulp Vs. The Throne puts the mic on the dead bird, the airlump whistling thighlike.
The Pulp Vs. The Throne names my pouchflesh L.L. BEAN.
The Pulp Vs. The Throne names my pouchflesh LAND'S END.
The Pulp Vs. The Throne sticks the liquid the ledges the thugmuffins.
The Pulp Vs. The Throne sticks the vowcolor the plots of stain the building pelts.
The Pulp Vs. The Throne hears silence as soon as it's in.
The Pulp Vs. The Throne the arrangement of the world trembles.
The Pulp Vs. The Throne the magic wrong responds.
The Pulp Vs. The Throne hears it say, MY YANKING POINT IS STRANGE.
The Pulp Vs. The Throne TELL ME I TAUGHT YOU TODAY.
The Pulp Vs. The Throne TRY TO.
The Pulp Vs. The Throne Can you explain everything stealing space?   )
The Pulp Vs. The Throne Can you explain why I'm healing?   /
The Pulp Vs. The Throne the magic wrong responds.
The Pulp Vs. The Throne hears it say, I'M READING SO MUCH ASHBERY.
The Pulp Vs. The Throne A Bulge is A Swell is A HEADDRESS.
The Pulp Vs. The Throne Can I shift and want in my HEADDRESS?
The Pulp Vs. The Throne flies out. To attend.
The Pulp Vs. The Throne cut to thoughts.
The Pulp Vs. The Throne cut to bloodvelvet.
The Pulp Vs. The Throne I don't care about dying, I care about energy.
The Pulp Vs. The Throne because calories.
The Pulp Vs. The Throne because pilgrim guts.
The Pulp Vs. The Throne because rinks.

The Pulp Vs. The Throne go-figure-
The Pulp Vs. The Throne go-figures-
The Pulp Vs. The Throne go-figure-it-out-
The Pulp Vs. The Throne spill bend stacks   spill force spill

HUMAN REFRAIN IS A GATHERING   / SPILL /
HUMAN REFRAIN IS A BRITTLE WHITE TRACK

                              spill underwear into your mouth

spill   into the centered / earth   and then turn it   spill it   until it is invisible

and a wet hurlplant   Still Blooming   behind your nearness

spill   where you are thrown by bore hounds
spill where they clamp down   and spring you out
spill where you are   so full of nearness to them   You Spill

        because being this mob surface it hasn't quite worked out has it

spill   exhaustion

        you tender clotted clutchhouse

      spill HUMAN REFRAIN It is in the middle   of my lovehands
      that say that say I have been thinking of writing to you in this way

/ I AM ORDER / FROM WORDS   / ARE THEY
COMING BACK / ON TOP OF ME   / red / G U A R D I A N L E S S?

When I say The Pulp Vs. The Throne,

                    I think of The Softness / Its Hardness, An Endlessness

and how it moves

                                        towards and maybe beyond a brittle Horizon, A Dilation

          mouthing A Distillation in preparation for swallowing it

There's Nothing Versus about A Boundary-Disabled Multitudinous

Shooting Spree Vs. The Simple Pleasure of Holding a Phrase Like

I Love You in Your Mouth.

The Pulp Vs. The Throne:

                              Can pearlmilk seep into row violence?
                              It does, and I watch the Dive closely.

The Pulp Vs. The Throne:

                              I watch the spongefisherman skin
                              as it collects the sea.

N describes to me   a scene   from A Film told in / Stills
/ in which the woman pulls her hair
/ to the top of her hair
/ to reveal her neck:

"It's terrifying because she is so exposed, she doesn't move. She can't move."

16

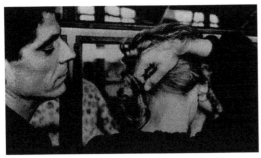

I ask how difficult it is to take and picture the River   at its wide
and widening point   I ask how difficult   it is to get the River its mesh

or its drone

                    or its boiling palace legs so gold
or its work
                    Between the two bonepoles of Earth   I think

I can be getting   everything them on me   between and I

am so slivered   Still   between and I   am so sharpened   Still
With one turned   apart flower,   I ask and get the round   for my hair

               A crown
               of hormone
               / and ruins

B l o o d on the wall
                     is also small

EXPAND HERE:

I feel in my mouth, a fingerprints.

I feel a strip ravel through granite:

How To Get Some Poems Written Being Who I Was.

How Irreducible Can I Be With The Violet Roof?
How Irreducible Can I Be With You?

(How / With Us
Is The Irreducible?
Into Seams / Where
Every Rehearsal /
Is To The Death.)

The Pulp Vs. The Throne,

The Pulp Vs. The Throne,   impossibility, impossibility, the unknown and its softgull
      runningthe   over and over, looping and looping, rehearsal, rehearsal,

repeating what shouldn't be,

      is my most fertile
      / is my most fur tiled land.

It has to be because fur is the most giving texture.
It has to be because paradox, p a r a d o x, p a r a d o x,

"A negative image from which positive pictures can be
created,"   says Anne Carson, "is a paradox."

That which not only shouldn't be, but CAN'T BE, is the thing that reproduces despite,

is the thing

that makes me feel DOUBLE.

I feel possibility because I am seizing

deep inside,

but I also feel thrive or shard

/ guilt or shame

trying to die trying to edit trying to die trying to edit trying to die trying to raw trying to glisten
trying to headdress trying to raw and to glisten and to headdress trying to die trying to edit trying
to die trying to edit trying to die trying to edit trying to die trying to edit trying to die trying to edit

because I am seizing so deep inside.

I farm and farm with a c i r c u l a t i o n   deep in something

that shouldn't or CAN'T BE.

Hello Fear. Hello Turning Horse   Desperate In The Frozen Space.

HELLO, I SMELL LIKE A MURDERVEST   CONTRACTION.

Doesn't it feel like you are creating problems where there aren't any?
Doesn't it feel like you are creating where there isn't anything?

There's me and the inverted flowers shattering under the sand.

\\\
****
\\\

I get a text in the middle of watching dead leaves.

N sends me a quote from Jacques Lacan, who
　　　　insists on "leav[ing] the reader no other way
out than the way in," which Lacan says he
　　　　"prefers to be difficult."

We are stuck IN language.

IN its obliterated DUNE FLOOR.

Subject: What is a building?

Dear J,
Dear Stickpack,

　　　It's storming, but I'm always bad at making myself close the windows. I almost typed cut the windows. Cut the windows off from sound and wetness. I'm soft for weather, though. When we were walking home, E said, "Are those clouds hugging that building?" And we laughed. The reason I brought up chartreuse and a bird in my message earlier is because last week I saw a crowd around a thing. It was a bird that had, moments ago, fallen onto the bridge dead or near dead. The color on it was turned up towards the crowd. They were all so young and concerned, and it amazed me? It seemed like a lost cause. They were trying to pick it up with a lid. But the thing is, E and I just now saw the bird crushed on the bridge, pieces and pieces of its brilliant belly smashed into the weird paint used to cover the ground. Did they abandon it? Did they give up? Did they lay it back down thinking…What? The bushes were so close by. It was as wonderful as it was bewildering, considering I had just used the bird and its color to write so quickly back to you.

The godbuck of pattern attuning in the middle of lush desert / blackberry, of pattern emerging to deplete distance,

this stance of difficulty and hoods

where there doesn't have to be any, where there could be ZERO,

of looping over all of them constantly.

'Being

                        [It's A LASH / A TINY CRAZE / Making
                        Out in The Grinding Over / I Would
                        Not Learn How to Remove]

The Pulp vs. The Throne is not an acknowledgement

                of approach that only fights against,

    but an acknowledgement of approach

                    in structures of soft collapse
                             / persisting,
                in a hood that dives off the wall
                          and into the water.

    What is the beginning of closeness until it confused the fraying planet?

    What is terror that decorates / me beautifully but terror?

    I look at pattern / chords / tightening, and I GIVE UP.

I want you,
your bonepoles,
and I am dying

                  because it opens up space
                  in me-my body, in me-
                  my name, in me-
                  my language.

enthroned," says Etel Adnan.

Did you like me when I die Did you like me
when I die when I mean to rip between
languages /

my lady / eats

my lady / eats

I've been to a rush lilac.
I've been to a wave of edge sorting
to what particle occurs beyond it.
I've been stuck in a full place.
I've been stuck in the place folding in on itself.

I've been to a rush lilac.
I've been to a wave of edge sorting
to what particle occurs beyond it.
I've been stuck in a full place.
I've been stuck in the place folding in on itself.

There is everyone at the lessening of your wounds,

but Repetition is never
Repeating Exactly.
It is each sentence Exactly.
Each sentence it is Exactly
what and where is Precise,
but what is Precise
Precisely if it doesn't
yield an Exactitude?

Maybe illegally,
it is / in French.

The scrape / or
cesspit thigh

of the word insists
on a trying
on a form
on a testing
on a making
on a repetition
by itself.

Each time round is an extraction.
Each time round we find the return.
Each time round the return is immediate.
Each time round the return is brutal.
Each time round the return is near.
Each time round I learn what should be a trap

: paradox
: impossibility
: repetition

is, because of poetry, always bringing me closer to you.

(powerlines)

(p o w e r l i n e s)

You, made of no light but noise.
You, made of questions of magnetism and gravity,

like any sentence.

I currantly call

I currantly call

and

I snap my gums

I snap / my gums

at a dry moon

II. BEING STONE

Being Stone,

The <3 ughs.
The <3 ughs.

Being Stone, when the liquid comes alive, I'm going to lie down in the wilds and grieve.

Being Stone, I'm going to lie down in the wilds

where WHO MATTERS it died,

where WHO MATTERS it devoted / it returned,

where WHO MATTERS it has / to put me down

in explicit texture,
in remain water,
in field injury.

I was put down in an OFFWORLD.
I was put down where I am marble and wet.

Being Stone, I'm going to lie down in the wilds

where no everyday lives / because fuck /

anything that doesn't know magic

is dreadful,
/ that it cares for bodies. /

Being Stone, I'm going to lie down on the matter / the salt / the curve / the drift bone / the drench jewelry / the blackest smartest / the bloom / the shell* / the ward / the cuff / the charm / the unwritten flexibility the water / slum the charnal / jellyflesh / the pelt / the scan / the collected dots / the sugar box / the bounty / the aggression / the glory roaring beneath me and tell you a joke.

*Can you send me some from the see-through jungle, c-horse? I'm craving it and might die otherwise, of sadness...Plz. Srsly? Plz.

-B

P.S. In the picture of the horse-tooth, your life line looks really great.

Being Stone, the lethal clouds.
Being Stone, I have the joke suspended by its lethal clouds.

Being Stone, why did the witch fly on her broom?
Being Stone, why did she pee dreams and fly?

Being Stone, when the liquid comes alive,
the answer is her vacuum was too heavy.

Being Stone, I feel climate is blood I feel climate is blood or it is by broke birth or is it by blood
I am excruciated Aren't you I feel climate is violet roof I feel climate I feel it blood and mutter.

Being Stone, when I am the liquid, it is about to coil.
Being Stone, I am going to die / I am going to call it Cherry.

Being Stone,

Who reads what comes to / on a wrapper?
Who reads what is basically a thin piece / of dirt string?
Who reads what comes to as an apparent slash?

Being Stone,

I wanted you to save my life stinging and
I wanted you to draw frames of me naked in saturation, hunting.
I wanted you to draw frames of me naked in saturation and universe froth, hunting.
I wanted you to draw frames of me naked in saturation and universe froth and ice flowers, hunting.
I wanted you to draw frames of me naked in tissue gowns above the mint drain.
I wanted you to draw frames of me naked in murals of ghost quit.
I wanted you to draw frames of me naked in tissue gowns eating the mint bread you unwrapped.
I wanted you to draw frames of me naked in unmade gangs of magnolia.
I wanted you to draw frames of me naked in figs and pressing draped over mint cliffs.
I wanted you to draw frames of me naked in golden and bleak forest / in bale draped over

mint cliffs.

Being Stone, you called me C-HORSE. You called me C-HORSE,
and I felt then that I loved you the most.

NS OF A STONE I THINK
K OF WHILE WRITING THIS:

1. The sack glass that changes hands?
2. The sack glass that sucks on your hands?
3. A receptacle for what is moving fast.
4. / A clot / A BLK MTN / A language
   that can't prevent certain forms.
5. Contamination status sparkling.
6. Contamination headdress sparkling.
7. There is tenderness that is rarely overcome.
   We are crushed,
8. fucked, or hitchhiked.
9. Fountaingrass urging over
   what peeled shut / Density / Distant Slit.
10. That swarm is alone and still a nurse.

Being Stone,

I'm eating a mango / my wealth.

Being Stone,

The slash / is me

trying to lie down//

Being Stone, we are encompassed.

Being Stone, Monster Stag,

a receptacle for what is moving fast,

a grid of sequins and fur that thought it would live,

says this is the instant stream.

This is the instant stream where you have wet self where / nothing's peace like an emotion.

Being Stone, Monster Stag and wet self and the instant stream curl up in the new wave.

/ I call them
Silk Butchers.

Being Stone, this is the initials

/ the initials from facing you with the idea that health is terrifying.

Being Stone, surviving the skin worn down to immersion is red buds softening.

Being Stone, the broth is drunk.

Being Stone, the broth of a small world trying is inside our bodies, which shudder.

What if less evaporated?

Being Stone, can I possess you?

Being Stone, you are not just the men I fuck in gorgeous / loved space.

Being Stone, we all fall apart more radically than that, disperse into slipping

back over THE FALLS, THE FALLS.

What if my absorption of you was powerful?

Being Stone, can I write to you?

Being Stone, what I send you will be outlined in red glitter as if I were a TREAT.

Being Stone,

What bursts forth is interference,
What bursts forth is a festival of betrayal.

Being Stone,

I make it tell the body profit.

Being Stone,

       what I want is for intimacy to expand

              and expand what it shouldn't be able to.

Being Stone,

       what's the worst thing I've ever done as a human being?

              The answer isn't human. It's Credit Card Debt.

Being Stone,

       what is a ceremony of approach?

I make from whatever happened / I make from something different that happened.
I make from the lodge petal / wrapping paper / I hold the Vaulted Footage in my arms.
On it we see: Figures / Long Sticks With Rag Hemorrhage On Top / Touch Fire.

Being Stone, C loves you.
Being Stone, what do you / do to C?
Being Stone, What does your voice / do to C, / tenderly?

The wild and high river gives the blood   nowhere to go   but up
into the living C's performance   on the page.

                 That world is so close.
                 That world is so close to romance.

Dear E,
Dear Wrecking Ball / Pendulum,

What are your fantasies about the poem?
I have so many RE: THE CRAMPED SPACE.
I have so many RE: THE OVERGROWN LINING.
What would you ask someone to bring?
What will I bring?
What are blocks and bricks and bubbles?
What is nonbearable?
When does the world know?

I want to call a hut / a light tent. I want to spike lemonade and have it molt off large pieces of fear in the event factory / in the velour nightground. Anything found / a soft skin.

I'm still awake eating strawberry from the cliff. I'm still vibrating and thudding thinking about L. Diggs ("Everyone wants to love / not many did it"), about slippery dance and healed burns and her perfect black button up, about when she called on you at the reading to make a sound / to be an apprentice to the inside and you said,

GOOOOOOOO BEEE DAHHHHHHHH.

I was sure I was watching your throat pull apart avocado. I was sure I was watching BLK MTN, bulky and sharp and wrong, unleashing anyway, unleashing the warm way we talked about forests of sex coming back from Iowa City, the way we talked through our draped skulls. I remember wanting to write on the inside of the wrapper (Do you remember the cheap candy I bought for us? It had that witch joke printed small on it?):

All I do is receive form. To mark the sensation in its place. Why there.

That sound you made? As an apprentice to the inside? I felt it unhook sack glass / hooves / the ramps / AN OVERLOOK from underneath / the sea / from underneath meat / or rather, from underneath a combination of the two / which is melt bloat / which is the weather outside right now. It's the spongefisherman suit covered in face portals and sinkholes and cheekbone and slick according to the drawing B sent to my phone / to our dream oil. I love that combination could mean a new mouthful or a secret pulse to space.

Are you on the porch? Are you on the shadow of community?

I came home from the reading and laid on the floor with N. The floor held together with animal rock. The floor held together with oyster. I laid on crystal plantation / it was hard and flashing. We talked what marginalized hybridity might be at its most excessive (I said, simply, that it was a llama) and about what it means TO BE FOUND threatening. How much pressure it is. How much rampage glimmers. What if it's turquoise? I HAVE BEEN FOUND threatening by real and imagined turquoise. The dirt underneath outside / the dirt underneath intense belly turns to turquoise. Or it turns / into a hole of homes.

It's difficult to sustain this kind of writing. It is difficult to sustain this poems / this HOT MASS as you like to call them / this RELIGION OF FLOWERS as I like to call them. When you opened your mouth without a coast, I thought of why I sometimes feel unsteady here inside this text, trying to make poems that are something other than total killing sound. Do you know what I mean? I knew when I made a killing sound, no one could ignore me. A body could refuse me. A body could not listen. But a body also couldn't help but HEAR me. I learned how to make a sound. Now I want to let sound give me the wetness to speak.

I think I overuse the word body, actually. I feel that dark cream whenever I go running and listen to Lisa Robertson. Where is the vernacular for *body*?

Ate some gluten-free cereal. / Now I own my first long skirt.

"A vernacular is the name for the native complexity of each beginner as she quickens," says Robertson. It gathers. It gathers by "wit, excess, plasticity, admixture, surge, caesura, the wildness of a newly turned metaphor, polylinguality and inappropriateness." I live in the stairwell, says B.

I like that.

I live in the changing turquoise. I live in the ribbon.

I hear N ask the question and then answer it.

—What do my words desire?
—They desire themselves.

I love you,

C

.

III. THE SILENT BONE

I'M A FIREHOUSE.
I'M A FIREHOUSE MADE OF BLK GLASS.
I'M A FIREHOUSE MADE OF BLK LABSS.

I get a panting feeling To feel the velocity

To feel the velocity   from a wedge   of cave.
To feel the velocity   from a wedge   of shortwakehole.

To feel how pressure allows   To feel how pressure allows
open strings To get to the water   To get to the water

I get a panting feeling To get to the water I get a lowermessweed I get

      used waves their / sliced hair They Are Lost In Their Own closeness

                OR their own hue
                OR their own interjection
                OR their own projection
                OR something more frightening
                than I have made before.

I get a gear blackness from being together.

I'M IN THE D(UGHhhh)OUT.
I'M IN THE CL(UGHhhh)B.

I don't know if I love anybody except that draped skulls key my skin into blossom.
I don't know if I love anybody except that my skin, it is in piles.
I don't know if I love anybody except that I call it The World's Extreme Corner.
I don't know if I love anybody except that I do,

except that I say over and over again, My hoist point my hoist point my hoist point,
and by that I mean, Lifting Out Of is what I have.

I dream like a hostage.
I dream like asphyxiation has cartilage.
I dream   and press

I dream and press my skivvies   over the water.
          They are rippling a little   however They Went Away.

You clutch something
wet. I kiss it
on the paint heel.

                    There is a crushing sound everywhere.

\>\>   I mow the lash.
I name it quietsunmotion.
I name it flushwitness.
I name my small girl John Deere the II. \>\>
I name her Deerest.

I mow the lash.
I have no choice.

In the dream, I am sitting

      down I am sitting down

when you w/ your clean shirt,
when you w/ your each finger

        in the sag of pigmentgrowth

     scream at me,

ARE YOU MADE AT ME?
ARE YOU MADE AT ME?

Subject: What is a shed?

Dear B,
Dear Softening Agent,

IN THE DREAM, IS IT HARD TO BELIEVE? I FEEL REDLIGHT IS
LIFESHORTENING TO A CLIP. I FEEL I AM CUT /

THE BUD / OFF THE BLOOD.

I am continually born from crisis. From fault lines. From poundage. From forces and the felt under-
neath. From block over me. From an impaired surface that pulls wool, fizzing, from panting roses.
From a lying down that carries. From the idea that the further I left it, the longer it went.

I am continually born from the idea that giving up on being an open, brave person is not an option.
From the idea that being an open, brave person is a necessary form of monstrosity.

Isn't a ribbon a towel? Isn't a ribbon a towel eating?

I stand very still and an accident walks right through me. I stand in smoke like it is coming off.
I stand in dome structures like it is coming off. A sentence overlaps with the job of opening animals
like it is sunset tracing itself a pulse named WINDOWLESS HEAVEN.

Sometimes I wish I wrote poems that could be the lapbones of fruit, the sand and the salt and the
leftover of casual worship. I wish I wrote the warmth collecting the valve.

In the dream, I was *Blow Ridden Blow Ridden Blow Ridden*. In the dream, I wrote it until something was
called posture. Has the possibility of beginning gently been near-dead?

I mean it in the most skin. I mean it in the drag of the padded envelope. I mean it in the chamber,
private and disgusting. In the dream, packed in edges ask. In the dream, packed in edges ask what could
get through. Are we each blocks being watched? What does travel them? What if it means too much?

Sometimes I look at the trees with their beautiful veins riversucking and feel like they should be afraid
of me. Sometimes I think poetry is afraid of me because I'm real. Because what I believe I write is
real. Is it dramatic to say something like that? Is it overly dramatic? But then again, that is creation.

But then again, what I am most afraid of are the people I love because they are real, because they
speak to me, because I need them so utterly to speak myself. I call them unimaginable people with
unimaginable power.

I started in the dumpsite where I was a poisoned flower burning alive.
I started in the dumpsite where I was the burst noise.
I started in a room soft of my cankerwash.
I started when my flecks were in a room soft of my single tree pinks

& y e s with-the-blade-down   a-forest-is-dripping.

I started when I had a dream in which Alice Notley pulled me out
wearing an Owl Skull smeared with blood.

She cried in people and in her knowledge.
I called it The World's Extreme Corner.
She said, Fuck You, Live Like The Startling You Lie Down On.

·

Last time I wrote to you, I said, Darkness Written on a Paper Fan. Last time you wrote to me, you said, How do you mend?

As I mend, I am able to document the fact that the sun will flip upside down in a couple of weeks. As I mend, I am able to document the subsequent flesh and light that will tear. As I mend, I am able to document my eyes crosshatched in gold thread. As I mend, I am able to document my life as a dung goddess named Snowblood with one cigarette left. As I mend, I am able to document my life as a [jut box] filled with tender ash. As I mend, I am able to document a jawstatue that shakes, a hungry ghost who wonders if there is such a thing as a massive sky. I believe in a massive sky. I believe it will have me mend. I believe in a massive sky that will teach the jawstatue how to blood and me how to grow Lightning That Touches A Beach And Makes Glass in the Versus, in the space that has already been sacrificed, in the space that is already so close to Verses. I believe in a massive sky. As I mend, I can leave language, and I can return to it. As I mend, I am able to chronicle, to be chronic in receiving, to be chronic in unspooling the rising thread that spreads between bodies *You* and bodies *I*, to be chronic in knowing the difference between transmitting pain and transforming it. As I mend, I call the lining between the fish and the sea electricity. As I mend, I wrap my groanvessel in tremendous waves.

Last time I wrote to you, I said, Or Suddenly The Hands Start Moving. Last time you wrote to me, you said, How does it make you feel?

I feel like Etel Adnan's pink dove who carries shattered human faces in her beak like pieces of coiled up cake. I am writing forward and into a continuum. I feel it peeling against me. I feel like blood chemistry eating a leaf. I feel, and I stand very still and nothing walks right through me. I feel like a sill is a cliff is an edge I lie down on. I feel like a black sun mating a red sun. I feel my portal mating another out of fear that they will die that way. I feel more like myself. What I feel, I said, when I was in lying in the back of a moving car in Cincinnati with my boots pressed against the window, is that to be against you is to be near. What I feel is that that is my elk bugle. Did you know that elk bugles sound like land dolphins? I turn around to feel N, who I love, take a picture of me smelling on my fingers, THE FALLS, THE FALLS. I feel like I will arrive. I am about to arrive, but I'm not sure if arrival is what they will call it. I feel the hospital of a rind glow. I feel the mushroom found in the collapsed levels of the rainforest that eats plastic. I feel like a fragment that is sticky. The fragment, says Elizabeth Grosz, must be "sticky" to attract, to attract other fragments. Sticky and Rough. I feel myself pulling out the property, pulling it out of myself. I feel myself proceed. I feel myself proceed via enactment and linguistic immanence into my crisis and into my bold river and into my massive sky and into my body and into your body. I feel myself and the difficult things and the magic things begin to flow into and on top of each other like bewildered area. To be against is to be near. To be against is to bring myself closer to you.

It's not just the air that's dismembered.

Does that thing going over the cliff go limp at any point?

The things I would die to have anyone hear.

I lay my head back in some water

and shake it from side to side like sanding.

I wish I had a stone to make me stop.

IV. DREADFUL CONTACT

I know the rest of the night will be as devoted to work as love as I'm now resting in this expensive sentence and in the end I'll spend it fast writing to you anyway, addressing you and a solution or night beginning like a letter, just a few words more freely seeing everything more clearly than the rest of life and love tends to be like windows facing mostly south but surrounding us, I'm thinking of you

—Bernadette Mayer

I LOOK AT YOU AND FEEL TOPLESS,

like a burn victim or a mermaid.

I write decay, decay, decay so I can
look at it and change my life.

Describe a morning you woke up without fear.
—Bhanu Kapil

I wake up on the cold of J's floor. *I have been thinking about you* His house is red and pouring with gaps that let full threads / The sun / exhalation / A boundary of ours in. I call my limbs raw nurses. I call them cruel thuds. *I have been passed by weather drowning a socket a clearing* His house is set back from the road. It's in a recess / a pause / it's so red / it's burning / during the while. *I have been c i r c u l a t i n g a socket a clearing* I wake up on the cold of J's floor without shrinking one hundred velvet spikes. *I have been thinking about writing to you in this way* How does the imperceptible element / an intercapillary patience / veilpiss / salt lovers become the site of species intensity? Frames open and / invention sends. / Frames open and / affiliation / or all ash faces up / approaches / from an unstable distance.

> Light coming through stone
> is an extraordinary event.

What if resistance floats immediately?

Without shrinking, I wake up describing.

Without shrinking, I wake up salt lovers

/ godlets

/ pink lightning

/ jellyfish

/ underwater bees.

Without shrinking, I wake up this container of hearts and stomachs.

Without shrinking, I wake up water / a dangerous cut loosed below.

Without shrinking, I wake up bulging jewels / or subsumed by my limbs.

Without shrinking, I wake up writing to you.

I am here. / I wrote it out again,

the intimately expanding memory,

the healing map swallowing a dead wood providing, from scratch.

Where did it go? How embarrassed am I by how I change? / By what?

The recess / the pause / the secret donor entrance. *I thought for a moment I never stop growing* I put on J's sweater and go outside to smoke one of his cigarettes while he keeps sleeping or puts welts of bread in a skillet. The sweater has diamond shapes and shedwater on it. Shades of / orange and green / or yellow that aren't dull / but neglected. J's house is so red / it's burning / during the while. *My unconditional presence in and around it* There are headstones pressed into the sides of it. Headstones, headdresses, I say to myself, dragging. *I feel warm I have lifted it by my pleasure* I touch the text / the seed / the marbles / the shift braided into the rock / into the animal rock / and think of how we (C and J) are in love with people (N and H) that are not us. I think of how we know it because we are still reading to each other. *It is not private / It can't be regulated* I think of how we know it because J asked me at the bar the night before. If I am in love with N. Yes, I said. Yes, and regenerating flowers suddenly blew up into

the vital arrangement of an admission.

IT WAS SO HOT /
AND IT WAS SO
HUMAN.

-What if writing down a name
-is a form of word choice / *my unconditional presence*
-*in and around it?*
-To make   a choice / *my unconditional presence*
-*in and around it* / To make a threshold I squat into /
-A contorted relaxation /
-is to follow   *the surrounding vibrational*
-as it creates / destroys / PILES on /
-as it atmospheres an unraveling.
-To write down your name and to follow it
-with Yes, is to think
-for a moment that I would never stop
-growing.

I woke up on the cold of J's floor and there was a text
message from N / WHERE R U? WHY AREN'T U
HERE?

It's hard for me to speak so plainly about the body

/ my friend

/ I have sex with my friends /

I still search for a wild god / J comes outside to join me /

                                        to join me We are talking when he / reaches over
/ to gather up my hair
/ to pull my hair to the top of my hair
/ to reveal my neck.

                    This vital arrangement

                        / This vital safety

my friend holds there
with his edible body
/ fastened grain
                        and skins.

                                        IT WAS SO HOT /
                                        AND IT WAS SO
                                        HUMAN.

Without shrinking, I say, What is a choke hold?

Without shrinking, I say, What is a chose hold?

Without shrinking, I say, I see a double kingdom choose over my mouth / the ground.

Without shrinking, I say, The ground is an earth candle.

Without shrinking, I say, It's an earth candle with dog necks / slanted into it.

Without shrinking, I say, Dog necks that ate at each other.

I try to rest at points. I go outside, and I try to put it on the ground. I try to put my devastation on the ground. I try to put it on the ground and pay it. My devastation, I pay it.

Dear J,
Dear situationroom,

Does rubbing have any ends?
What is a corridor of peaks and does it dangle inside me like snow?
What is the difference between chaos and territory?
I'm touching clay and connecting it to the work to be.
Which flower do you gravitate towards?
"I threw away my shoes looking
for you on the throat
of a flower"
This is from a poem I sent you,
but I don't know who wrote it.
Why do you think they did it?
"And I live in the vague
terror you will call and offer me a summer song and a coffee."
Why do we offer ourselves?
Where is rareness?
Do you remember the New Year's I wrote to you
and said, I left someone. I did. I did. I did. How could I? Am I full /
Am I full of nothingness / Heavily so?
Do you remember when we stood outside
/ and my hair was disturbed
by the healing event / The sun / exhalation / A boundary of ours?
I understand waking up / Here is the slaughter of sequence / A floral /
they can always be reshaped and sometimes
that is so IT for me.

Dear J,
Dear situationroom,

Inexperienced change makes me

                    / Inexperienced change

          MAKES ME LAUGH / MAKES ME SWOLLEN

                    DOES IT YOU?

From The Garden of The Blue F.U. Dogs:

Dear Carrie,

I started reading *Bluets* tonight. I'm ¼ done already and it's late but
I feel the need to finish it now. I was starting to feel the full weight
of the book when Kelin texted me that she loves me, was reading
umbrella essay, and hoped I was in a good moment. Or "on the verge."
Then I separated all of Abby's letters from my other letters, tied them
in a bundle, and stood there not knowing what to do with them.
Why should I be telling you? It sounds like I'm hung up. I'm not. But
Bluets loosed something. I see what you mean. I am listening to Jason
Molina by the green horse. When I sat down to the letters I found this
postcard and knew to write you. Maybe, selfishly, to salvage something
of myself. "It's true it was a hard time I come through / But I'm still
thankful for the blues."

Love, N

WHAT R U / WHERE R U
SHACKED FLESH / RECKLESSLY
SLOW / ON MY HUMAN SKIN?

Work lay / work was in a spreadable wire
And positioned above it was a word /

How do I moor
/ *love?*
Why would I?

Work lay / work was secured by material

that could be crushed beneath a body /

folded gently and precariously

just from the weight of itself.

How do I several
/ scary light

light

light

light?

WHEN I LOOK AT YOU, I BLANK OUT

activated.

PUBLIC EXCESS CHANNELS

'So what if she is thick and stupid behind her life. It is not private.'
'It can't be regulated.'
'No, it is a survival, a learning-to-live.'

—Lisa Robertson

FEAR IS THE
BEGINNING OF
DEVOTION / OF
A DEDICATION

-To poetry.
-To the color Red.
-To the color Red / collected outside
-/ dry stems.
-To flowers.
-To garlands / sentences.
-To headdresses.

-"To a body of infinite size there can be ascribed neither center nor boundary."
- Myung Mi Kim

Fear[1] is the beginning / of devotion / of a dedication.
It's the beginning of a need and a desire to be devoted.
A need and a desire that emerges
/ becomes apparent
/ becomes an apparition[2]

                                    when I'm throwing myself,
                  circuits blowing,
                  spraying
                  / painful rocks
                  / jewels
                  / or sea glass,
                                    into a ditch.

Into a soft spot.
Into a shallow puncture in the ground.

"Beginning wherever you like, tell even us." —Theresa Hak Kyung Cha

---

1 "Do you know what I've / been through? Was it ever / worse for you? / Or I could say, This corpse is / the one you killed. And you'd / gape at me. / If I say it to myself, what's / that? that I killed it? / Maybe I killed the whole / thing." —*Songs and Stories of the Ghouls*, Alice Notley
2 I am a conjurer. / I am conjured.

I fear when the earth formed.
I fear when the earth is formed.
I fear when it formed by those
/ who would have me killed.

We were Creatures We are Shifts.
Do I need to name them,

                  the cave-hunters / ?? /

Don't you know /

                  the cave-hunters / ?? / Firm Tones / Violent Street Mud

/ The Face Traveling
/ A Public Groping Slits Out / The Moon
/ Fatty Haunted Gold
/ I throw myself into a ditch.
/ Gutter Butter
/ I'm naked for earth Art.

        Into soft spot.
        Into a shallow puncture in the ground.

                A dedication:

                        You're in the place I called us to.

        You're something.
        You're something
        palatial and precise.

                    "A no-space of extremity, without inhibitions, lifted."
                      —Stephanie Young

I wrote this out of fear.
I wrote this out of fear that made me flourish

and take oil across the mood
rings on fire.

But all I'm going to do tonight
in the fucksnow,[3] /
in the glittering
or discarded sunlight,
is throw myself.

Throwing myself is diving for lovers.[4] The act of throwing myself, in writing or in my physical
form, requires possessing only enough control over an out-of-control body to move it / in a last
ditch effort.[5] In an unusual intensity / I throw myself into the wound / the opening so that I
might take cover. There is cover / a surfacing that doesn't result in my being utterly buried or lost.
I'm thinking / towards safety / rather than protection. Safety still considers risk / Takes it. There
is cover / a surfacing that still involves air and very deep breathing[6] / the blank part of the page
surrounding me, but not burying me.

> I have the breastcage of a horse
> when language comes over me,
> codelike / botanical.

---

3 / A TEXT FROM E: "IN THE FUCKSNOW WITH RUM AND PONIES."
/ A TEXT FROM E: "CHANGE THAT TO IN THE BITCH ICE WITH TEQUILA AND HORSE
EGGS."
/ A TEXT FROM RON PADGETT AND JOE BRAINARD: "HERE / IT IS LATE / AT LAST / AS
USUAL / I'VE FUCKED THE DAY THE / DAYS AWAY."
4 I throw myself at you / hair wide.
5 "Get a glass of rum / With a gun and some pun pun / Oh fun fun fun" —M.I.A.
6 The feeling I have on bridges / which I have always been afraid of / open aired / exaggerated connector
space / lofted and dangling / hanging dangerously swaying / on a forceful day / in the wind. The graffiti I
can see from the bridge spells out, ACHE.

Engulfed by fear, I am floating / on my back or stomach in the swelling conditions / of a ditch turned / river. I am floating in the matter we live in.

Engulfed by fear, I simultaneously go blank and begin regrouping / regenerating. A misty / veil Alp / or an ever-loving paradox named survival.[7]

This not only becomes monotonous / but becomes incredible.

7 What is it to make it through language's impact constantly? What is it to live through reading? What is it to live through inscription? Do you feel it? These questions are so present* in me, so vivid in their consistent throbbing. I'm afraid no one believes me. I'm afraid they'll laugh.

*"The text's social address: Its immediacy to our senses helps to produce a Real, not to concoct an incorporeal simulacra of theatrical presence." —Bruce Andrews on Gertrude Stein

"WE CAN'T NOT DIE FOR EACH OTHER," I say by accident in N's living room.

In the midst of taking cover / a surfacing, I perform a kind of tension as language leaves me / comes over me, codelike / botanical. I find myself with the power / to paint like a dead flower person / to linger in what I don't know, in what I am coming to know. Do I have the ability to move? I languish in pieces of stretching.[8] I find the standing water / when I am laying down in it.

Flowers come over me, little purses / little receptacles of pollen and intimate that collected in the run-off, in the marginal water / soil space, and I perform a kind of tension that's electric in its devotion to the surrounding area. "I want to think about that tension," says Elisabeth Workman, "as one of ferocity." Lozenges in the soil / teething. Little shoots / about to suck the bloompoison out of a deserving event. What is it to deserve in an event? By that I mean, what is it to proceed in an attention? To feel it in you as it moves / breaks / experiments?

> Fear might be the ability to tear apart.

> (WORD-FIRES)

> Fear might be the ability to tear apart.

---

8 B and I are on our way to a free dinner at the university. We are going to steal a feast / in our gold suits. We create stores / with the feeling of / constant begging.

I understand that part of the tension I'm talking about and performing with regards to fear is that what I've gathered to myself for analysis or rearrangement emerges from seeing / I'm something to fear. I've discovered[9] I'm something to fear. I find that I'm something to fear, and I begin to understand that what I am is a threat.[10] It's a process[11] of realization that haunts and unsettles this continuum of writing, which only further causes the writing to thrive / to feel "departmentalized shame."[12]

---

9 What if discovering you're a threat is part of the unexpected language, the creation / the launch in the poem? This isn't the conversation that revolves around writing that is considered to be causing or suggesting shifts within instances of writing / poetry. What if you never wrote anything meant to disturb anyone, but came to understand that it might disturb someone(s)? Should I replace disturb with hurt? How does that alter you?

Change* is not an attack, though violence often erupts around it, / surrounds it, or occurs.. Change / Transformation is a living movement. This is not to say the edges aren't there, that they aren't a texture that can be felt / that can cut. This is only to say that those edges are mutable, that our attentions can evoke or receive an awareness of that malleability.

*"Chris Kraus says 'Anne Rower says when you're writing in real time you have to revise a lot. Writing is a mode of living / movement. By this I think she means that every time you try and write the truth it changes. More happens. Information constantly expands.' And she said that in 1996. What's real time?"
—*Ursula or University*, Stephanie Young
10 "Don't fuck with me / Don't fuck with me," sings Jai Paul in disarming / falsetto. "I never knew where I was goin' / I went where the water was flowin'."
11 "With minimal gestures, the time of my sensing is repeatedly annexed." —*Nilling*, Lisa Robertson
12 Lisa Robertson

When I'm writing / I mishear the line in the Jai Paul song
as / "THAT SHIT WAS THE LOVE OF MY LIFE."
/ I think of poetry / and try not to cry.

> "Nobody including you
> Of all the people doing things, was approving"
> —*Midwinter Day*, Bernadette Mayer

"How preoccupying
Is the wish to include all or to leave all out
Some say either wish is against a poem or art

I'm asking

Is it an insane wish?

To be besieged, beset with,
To have to sit with, to be harassed, obsessed,
To be possessed or ruled by

I am confused by

Fear, perfection and love, this poem,
Order, mourning, vigilance and beer
And cigarettes and directness
Of clarity, words, truth or writing
Or the sublime

Everyday

These apologies are what they call under control
I've no respect for their repetitious logic
And though I'm obsessed with keeping track

Of where you are in the house or out of it
I rarely clean it thoroughly"
—*Midwinter Day*, Bernadette Mayer

"'What have we" "to do" "with the tyrant?'" "said a woman" "'He some-
how keeps us here" "but in my life I" "must have my life,"
"must squeeze my life out of" "being here" "Must be here" "since I
am'" "She was crying" "A dark woman" "large-

faced" "comfortably fleshed-out" "Her eyes" "shut the tears in"
"then opened" "again"
—*Descent of Alette*, Alice Notley

89

In this space where I am / permissive, I recognized that I couldn't say, I'm going to write a poem. Instead, in this space where I am, I have to reach / I have to say, I'm going to write in the poem. I'm going to fail you, / the warmth of bodies, / their consciousness, through a choice. "Choice guarantees murder," says Edmond Jabès while I'm writing. The force / of the water that holds them all / shifts / dreams the sun / the drawing of language / the drawing of language / the blood etching / which is the thing / that can hold frenzy / that can hold tumult.

I didn't know how to continue, only that I would / and agape.   / O, / I use my lungs loyally. / I want to be pursued.   / I want to pursue, / I do.

I wrote this out of fear for how I would continue / to resist writing a poem
        / so that I could write a poem.

                        I pressed against / something. / I opened something.

I had to grate myself into the room / to learn speaking.

Once I opened the poem / I had to face it
/ I had to face the possibility

            / that none of the forms feel big enough,[13]

 / that I won't stop growing,

/ that I will fail to stop growing / beyond what is proper / what is the property.

/ Wildflowers
/ Flower Thieves.
                "To transgress but then to come back, and to come up with a syntax
                that feels like that feels,"
                                says Selah Staterstrom.

There is compassion in transgression / in resistance / in movement.
How has it touched us?

---

13 Presidents / their ebbless wars. Me / my ebbless mouthfeel / fingertips / pussyfeel.

This is the point where I find myself turning away from the line between poetry and anything else, where I become a face in the other direction, shimmering.[14] This is the point where I give myself the dimensions that allow / for dispersion that doesn't feel far away / from each other. I raid dimensions that allow for patience, for co-recognitions spreading through a body, / a bounty of work, / the determined and reaching claims of a BLKTHROAT. The raid occurs in a luxurious spiral, in velvet piles of squatting. I ripple through the twisting sand and blood of the poem. I learn speaking / and grow exposed / to the circulation and life of statement. How that might have something to do with realizing our intentions, strangely, despite ourselves.

I want to meet statement with our life and our imagination.[15]

This is the point where I understand an act of writing, / an act of trying, in the hope that I might speak, is possessed by fear that what will be created will repeal bodies, / their warmth.

Desire or demise, it says in effervescent blue clots on a wall in Atlanta. "The blue things I treasure are gifts, or surprises in the landscape," says Maggie Nelson. I look at it and say to myself, What's going to happen to me?

14 "...ultraviolent in a good way. The violence of stepping out of one life and into another, with the freedom to mourn, love, and create works of art that nobody can resist" —Bhanu Kapil
15 Here, intensity and urgency balance each other through an embrace / Toil Rod / I took a photograph with my whole body / It crumbled / boxes of Snow / It wrapped up in me / in order / to increase the velocity.

What if I sicken you with an exuberance?[16] With my compulsions?

To be repugnant / To be a pug in a headdress.[17]

Vomiting flowers are talking, speaking. I have read it / Dark Castles.

"Deserts of love," Zurita says, and then he repeats it.

The violence of a desire to emphasize. To come across despite.

I have written to you / with so much bound up in it.[18] I am thinking about you. I have felt it in the expressions of faces trying to face me / my repugnance that is part of facing me. Am I a good girl or a bad girl?[19] I answer the question by asking what strength is exactly. I don't want what is necessary to me / to hurt you / to be a capacity / for cruelty.

16 "I can't get my exuberance under control, it's more volatile than my rage." —Joyelle McSweeney.
17 "In an art class, my teacher asks me what I think a self-portrait is. I don't know why I can't answer gently. I don't know why my music only subtracts and doesn't know how to add / I get carried away by music and disappear into the supersonic," says Kim Hyesoon. "It's a pug in a headdress," I answer. "It's something beautiful and aware of contortion, of the disfigurement / the improvisation that comes with crawling over* / a growth. This kind of flowering is the body of the world. We're going Over Seas, / but closely."

*"The airplane passenger sees only how the road pushes through the landscape, how it unfolds according to the same laws as the terrain surrounding it. Only he who walks the road on foot learns of the power it commands, and of how, from the very scenery that for the flier is only unfurled plain, it calls forth distances, belvederes, clearing, prospects at each of its turns." —Walter Benjamin
18 Capaciousness is what E called it, outside with a cigarette / in the Spring / wetter. I'm leaning against a wall while we talk / #capaciousness. A hashtag is the pound sign, is a grid / a crust of sensation working its way to the surface. It's a protrusion.
19 Am I a short echo? / Am I Hollaback Girl? / OOoohH this my shit / this my shit. "I'm a popstar and this is how I feel," says Lisa Robertson. "#GETITRIGHT," says Miley Cyrus. Giant Bearings / Their Panties.

Is that an inversion of devotion? A painful one.

The small hair on bee legs makes me think of the crunchy seawater of figs,

which B calls inverted flowers.

In the margins, M writes,

Don't you have to feel a little threatening to feel others feeling you?

UNDERLINE THE ONE THAT SPEAKS

                         TO YOU

UNDERLINE THE ONE THAT SPEAKS

                         TO YOU

      / Dedicate to a soft horizon

      / a curb

      / with so much bound up in it

SOMETHING LIVES HERE / A SOFT HORIZON /
WITH SO MUCH BOUND UP IN IT /

UNDERLINE THE ONE THAT SPEAKS

                         TO YOU,

    IT LIVES
              / OR IT IS ROSES

-To a raw heart

           / its irregular pearls.

-To a healing

           / its irregular worlds.

-To a wreckage

           / its listening. To spending a million dollars
-on a crying jag. To a relentless Being / called U. To an initiation / A piece of Cloth
-from the brink / a crucial point I wore in / The beginning/ like a Bulb or a muscle

TO LIE DOWN /
IN AN ATTEMPT

"[An] ill-conceived repose on the edge
of the flood, so that looking down into it one no longer saw
the comforting reflection of one's own face and felt secure
in the knowledge that, whatever the outcome, the struggle
was going on in the arena of one's own breast. The bases
for true reflective thinking had been annihilated by the
scourge, and at the same time there was the undeniable
fact of exaltation on many fronts, of a sense of holiness
growing up through the many kinds of passion like a tree
with branches"
—John Ashbery

/ Y the ground / Y a body Y / a cuff / Y posture Y a thousand grindburies Y a thousand

                                  raw disintegrating mounds / IF U PLANNED THE DISAPPEARANCE
OF MY DESIRE / IF U MEET IT U WILL HAVE TO / LET IT WALK
        THROUGH / U OR U WILL /

                HAVE TO LAY DOWN IS THERE AN ACCIDENT IS THERE
      A FIRST TIME I WANTED / TO EXPLAIN CLEARLY

IS THERE ANOTHER PART OF THE TEXT / OF TALKING
             AS CLOSE AS IT CAN COME / IS IT LAVENDER CLAY IS IT
             LAVENDER AND RED CLAY ON THE VERGE OF ROSES /
IS IT A DREADKNOT /
DOES THE WORLD FORGET A BODY / A CUFF A THOUSAND COMPRESSED
       THERE / DELICACIES W/ A ROUNDED EDGE THERE SAYING,
 "U WAIT." /
            REPEATING THEMSELVES BESIDE IT / BESIDE THE WORLD
IS THERE AN ACCIDENT IS THERE /

            A STEM / I WANTED TO
      IMPLODE WRITING OR CONFESSION OR SOFTENING INTO A PRESENCE
    / INTO AN ESSAY PRECEDING ALL OF ME / A HYBRID CRUSHING
    / A DREAM WITH A RIVER / THAT ALSO PHOTOGRAPHS ME THAT /
ALSO SPLAYS ME FUCK U

I'M A BOOK OF LIFE AND OUT

FUCK YR LYRIC AS *YOUR* LYRIC / I'M A BOOK OF LIFE AND OUT

/ I'VE BEEN HAUNTED / I'M UNLEASHED
/ I'VE BEEN HAUNTED   / BY ORANGEPEELS / FOUND FIRESIGNS
/ READING PAST DUSK / ALL SPRING / ALL SPRING I PICK ORANGEPEELS UP
OR PHOTOGRAPH THEM AND SAY,

HOW CAN I BE SO MATURE IN THE DAY TIME
AND TOO IMMATURE IN THE DARKNESS / ALL SPRING AND ALL COARSENESS /

I'MMA TEXTURE / BETWEEN STABILITY AND VOLITION AND FLOWERS /
       Y THE MONARCHS THEIR ORANGESKINS THEIR ORANGE SEGMENTS R
DISAPPEARING / Y THE DEAD AREN'T RETURNING / Y YR LAWN IS A SERIES OF
STERILE CAMPING   / MOVING IN NOTHING THERE IS NOTHING TO STEAL
/ THERE IS NOTHING TO NOTICE THE MOUTH WITH
                       / Y THE PUBLISHED MOUTH FEELS ME

   / I STEAL THE LOVE THAT ATE THE FLOWER
   / THAT ATE THE VERGE
   / THAT ATE THE SHEER PRESSURES DRAGGED BY LAUGHING OR
       WEEPING   OR FUCKING I AM ALMOST A FUNCTION OF THEM /
       OF THE LOVE THAT ATE / THE GHOST CANYON

                       / I LIE DOWN IN WHAT I STEAL / I STEAL TENDER
AS AN EAGLE / AS A BIRDBLOOD
       I STEAL TENDER AS LOVE CROWDS / A SAND $ / A WOUND SOUND
       / AN ABSOLUTE BOUNDARY OF SENTENCES / PINNED AGAINST THE SEA
FOAM / AS BRIGHT AS BLACKBERRIES / AS DEMANDING AS TENSION.

       / IF U MEET IT U WILL HAVE TO / LET IT WALK THROUGH / U

       A GARDEN / IS A TANGLE / THE WORK OF A GARDEN / IS A TANGLE
       / A BODY / A CUFF / A GARDEN IS ON THE GROUND AND ALSO LIFTING
AWAY FROM IT / BLOOMING AWAY FROM IT
       / I WANT TO SAY IT IS A PERFUME BUT I CAN'T STAND PERFUME / BUT
I AM ALSO TRYING TO RETURN / BUT I AM ALSO THROWING MY SKIRT UP / BUT
RIMBAUD ALSO SAYS IT ENDS / IN A RIOT OF PERFUME /

98

IT ENDS

IN AN ANNOUCEMENT OF PRESENCE / A RESISTANCE /

To resist is to become commodious / a false indigo

To resist is to bring myself closer to you. I LIVE WITH YOU NOW / I BUY US BEER AND KISS US / CERTAIN IT IS WILD. I feel / unsightly / I don't mean ugly, / I tell E in a letter, I mean unpicturable. / I DON'T MEAN UGLY, / I MEAN

UNFATHOMABLE. How much am I accused / of searching for something / that is unavailable? / To resist is / to invite in what isn't expected, / to then do something familiar with it / ?? / to then do something unfamiliar with it / There are just roses when I think What if it's pure feeling / ?? / "We are Naturalists of the inessential," says Lisa Robertson, in an essay about an invasive blackberry (*Rubus Armeniacus*). "*Rubus* shows us how to invent."

To resist is to acknowledge a connected complex, a difficult witness, a dumb abandoned beach[20] house that doesn't say / but evokes pussy, pussy / in the water inclined / in the water reclined.[21] "To be explicit is a privilege,"[22] says Bhanu Kapil. You are a living, I say to the water. A LIVING.

To resist is to re-incorporate, to re-position, to move while re-visiting, / to move while reading / the writing, to move while living / the writing. To resist is to pull you closer / through the creation / of an excess of boldness. To resist is to pull you closer / through the creation / of an excess of surface / for us to lie down together on.

To resist is to collapse.

---

20 "The birth of Venus happened when she was ready to be born, / the seawater did not mind her, and more important, there / was a beach / not a breach in the universe, but an actual / fucking beach that was ready to receive her / Shell and all. / Love and food of" —*The Heads of the Town up to the Aether*, Jack Spicer
21 I'm overcome by pleasure/pain / pleasure / pain / the next thing I'm going to write.
22 "If I hear the word privilege one more time, I'm going to shoot myself in the head," says the Male Professor. E and N and I go out back to smoke and be pissed / eat. It isn't Hell because it isn't difficult to tell people from other people. E and I bury an empty bottle of champagne in the flowerbed. N puts on Anne Blonstein's dress, a wide sack of prairie. He picks a card from the tarot deck. It is The 8 of Rivers, the dancing shaman, the unknown singer, the circling water.

I am sitting
/ peeing
/ thinking
/ holding
Ashbery's *Three Poems*
/ thinking of how I want to write about lying down as some kind of rejection of the face, /
        of the face alone, / a proportioned reflection
(the ease / the trash / the chemicals of the reflecting pool)
/ in exchange for seeing the massive sky. /

              The reflecting pool won't teach me how to be resumed
              / how to be ravenous / an impulse of slits / a sea-wolf soft
              with onion or apple / soft with a contracting / ??? / a contraction.
MIRRORS R AN OBSTACLE,
              I say to the tiny flower with a huge question mark written on it.

I thought I didn't remember any of the book, / just the feeling of reading it / out loud / out loud against / my apartment's wood floor / just the feeling of it, / a copper thread / a departure gallery. But when I re-read the page where the word "flood"[23] is underlined, where "[an] ill-conceived repose on edge of the flood" is underlined, I realize I've been practicing thinking of the book / its insides / all along in my writing / in my life. To hold the text / with my insides To remember / with my body. What does that mean? This is the most important kind of reading I've only just learned how to do. The reading I do away from the book. The reading I do while feeling or looking at the text elsewhere and beyond. The reading I do / how prone I am to dog / and cake / and compulsion / and a mosaic or bristling / nudeness Am I poet Aren't I mere / mutilations?

---

23 UNDERLINE THE ONE THAT SPEAKS TO YOU.

When I lie down,[24] I no longer
catch the reflection of my face.
I see the massive sky.
I Still / hear the water see
                    ,

what my body remembers.
It is a situation of seeing /
lying in the dirt,
lying on the cliff,

                              sticky with ice. / A wet perch,[25]
          / it colors.

          "a sun ??? yellow ??? a ??? sun ???
          green ??? a ? boat ? blue and pink"
          —*The Arab Apocalypse*, Etel Adnan

                         What does a corpse mean where you are?
                         asks B in a letter. I wonder what corpses mean in
                         Florida? Have you ever seen
                         a corpse.
                              Whatever it is they are, it's also burned?

---

24 Would I die* / ** for poetry? Yes.

* "Existence as an intervention in the surface tension," —*Transfer Fat*, Aase Berg Trans. Johannes Goransson

** Wedged in the center of Frank Stanford's *The Light the Dead See* is a scrap. / It says, "The hoopoe, Ye-
hoahim thinks," / —*The Heart is Katmandu*, Yoel Hoffman. (I have always read it as, "The hope, Yehoahim
thinks.") / Underneath that / it says, "J, Order a book, and I will write a note to you in it."
25 A wet perch / A welt A porch / *Umwelt* / *Umwelt* / *Umwelt* / *Umwelt* / *Umwelt* / *The Stone is Not Worldless
Here* / *The Surrounding Worlds Put Flowers on The Ashes of Each Other* / *To Make Stones Stuffed With Inhaling Skin* /
The Surrounding Worlds Ruined Each Other / *Umwelt* / *The Surrounding Worlds Water a Torrent of Flowers* / *Until They
Bleed Fire* / *Through Their Spit* / *The Stone is Not Worldless Here.*

There's a body. Unquotable / Remarkable.

It's unquotable / so instead, it's remarkable.

Does it understand resistance / or is it a moving hole / of /
bones and ambition / lying so Still / or absorbent?

Mostly what I mean by Lying Down is that /
The weight of things is actually a greatness
/ A great joy for me.

"Because I'm moved in writing to be irrepressible.
Writing to you seems like some holy cause, cause
there's not enough female irrepressibility written
down. I've fused my silence and repression with
the entire female gender's silence and repression.
I think the sheer fact of women talking, being,
paradoxical, inexplicable, flip, self-destructive but
above all else public is the most revolutionary
thing in the world"
—*I LOVE DICK*, Chris Kraus

It's raining I wanted to study It's pouring / the rain buckles I wanted to study THE FALLS THE FALLS / the water buckles venting a spray A Wave I wanted to study / "Glittery and bridal," / says Bhanu Kapil I wanted to study Bhanu / The champagne or ribbon of her lying down / O Ban, / I write next to you / I write next to choking roses / Countries / Our bed sheet dipped in wax / when I'm lying down I'm swaying / U read something until it is there in U / Bleeding Horses Are Flowers, I say when We're at the beach / Pressing my Forehead into the sand / the broken Mating the sore shell / O B, O Ban, / What is derangement? Are there streaks of green / Blushing / Rapidly? A mutation flows into attracted spaces / into luminous forms / into collapse / into re-centering / the earth Art. The "or so / the or so—" at the end of the line in Brandon Shimoda's O Bon / is so Tender it makes me cry / an opened knot / a dash / is a grave / Can't I get my arms around it? / I can't. / "You lie down. Down. You do not realize you are disappearing," says Edmond Jabès. / No, no What if it's not disappearing but joining A complexity of disappearing and reappearing? / "(He'd always called her the group)," / says Michael Earl Craig in a book called / *Talkativeness* / living Rain is coming / A million intersecting poems The beach shows it intersecting Close by / Right now, It's burn your deep necked Robe / weather in Paris / "Sorry for the French goodbye / You're welcome for the French hello," / says Dana Ward, "Crying" / I love the smell of tomato plants most, says B. Pleasure / and Poison / and Eyelashes. In weeping I flood / so much Water So much water doesn't fight It Floods / It's a Long Unarmed population / I sit on N's chest while it rains enough / to get dark early and cry / I sit on N's chest and say, I feel / I am Abandoned[26] I am Discarded by this Poem / A Moving Hole / of Champagne or Ribbon / In the Woods you Wanted Me / The Jewel Thief / The Crawlfish / Losing her Pendant / her French for Duration / in A Forest of guns that doesn't say Spring is Breathing / that crying is breathing I wanted to study / that lying down is breathing I wanted to study / I wake up, and it's raining / No one believes me / that I'm dressed like Jane Goodall today / "I grab my chest during an argument," / N reads Bernadette Mayer's *Utopia* to me over the phone / the Jungle is Special / The Jungle a lighthouse near / The Gulf A Forest of guns / Flexible resistance to terrible things / Flexible limbs to gushing Sugar / to gushing / Proof / I weep thirst I weep trying to lie down / with you You're talking to love I wanted to study / "Water, water is a mountain and it is selected and it is so practical that there is no use in money," says Gertrude Stein about / "Sugar" / Your voice changes when you lie down, says M / Tomato Soup in her hands / "A yellow sun eternal vertigo in my hand," says Etel Adnan RE: Lying Down / I'm lying down in my hands No page numbers / only bit up wedges are a person / J calls me and asks if he

26 "Then she reaches a point where she can name her own death. She accepts the conception of death which is similar to painful childbirth. At that moment, somewhere within her, she can feel a sense of opening of a woman's world that has the hearing of death. She is hearing the femininity....In the world of hearing, she learns that she is more conversational and performative. In the numerous repetitions of the symbolic processes, the going back and forth between the inside and the outside, through this spiral process, she discards the identity imposed on her and begins to feel the transformed identity she now has—the identity coded by a different method." —*Princess Abandoned*, Kim Hye Soon Trans. Don Mee Choi

can read to me / The Whale / It's a Tunnel Made of Drowned Breathing / Sugar Breathes during Dates / under the Palms laid Down / anyway / N[27] calls me and asks if he can read Alice Notley to me / I Must Have Called and So He Comes / "There's this place in us," he says, "the so-called pain can't get to like a shelter behind those spices – coffee and sugar" / "We don't say pain we say fucked-up," Ted says, / N cries reading Alice Feeling / devoted to her / to me / to C / to poetry / to the Canon Fucking / to a Canon of fucking A future I remember / Dana Ward Crying While Reading his poem for Alice / I was just crashing the Class / My shirt was Black with Flowers / on A's bed / Yr Last Day as a Student should be like this / N and I keep saying / we taste it on each other We are derivative / of diamonds and cigarettes lying in the earth / Art It is like this, "A vast wetness as of the sea and the air combined"[28] / Take out the "as" / to get rid of any metaphor I cry / I cry because it has been A Dedicated Rain / I grab my chest because sometimes I'm jealous of other women I love / of the other C / of N / but Flowers, Hear me / I lie down in flesh chalk I wanted to study / in language / My Devastation my love of Men and rain and Jewelry / By Jewelry I mean Colored / branches terrorizing / a Canyon I lie down on / in swarms By Jewelry I mean, "This image knew no bounds"[29]

---

27 "I'm working out the structures of men that don't exist yet," Ted Berrigan says in "Easter Monday," a poem / of lines told in quotes / " "/ on the page like Alice in *Descent of Alette*. I look at the page / while I'm writing / and want to lie down on it with / these men that now Exist / "There is ultimately an inadequacy to everything I think & this fills me with extraordinary hope"* For us We / go thinking is Insane Wishing / longing / We go thinking did the universe ever welcome us / R Wet Crotches / R Deliberate Crotches / R For Us / R Rooting For Us / I believe that I do / I am the Football Player in this relationship, says M in a text / I believe her I do / Because She is a Delicacy / a Difficulty / a Shift / a Quiver. For us We / R Being / the antlers of bodies together on a Cliff / The Ghost Canyon Flooding / the Deserts of love. N and I, we watch the Horse Flower in front of us toss its head into Traffic, while Alice cries for the first time. I'm weeping now. Fuck YR memoir I'm alive / I'm sorry I feel so Strongly against it / but it doesn't want me to be alive. Deserts of love, says Zurita. He says it twice. I repeat you to myself. What is the most lying down / in our species / Their fields? ACHE, says my book, my shattering cheek.

*—"Typing Wild Speech," *This Can't Be Life*, Dana Ward
28 *Three Poems*, John Ashbery
29 *Schizophrene*, Bhanu Kapil

A LETTER IS AN UNREGULATED GLAMOUR /

JULY 30 – AUGUST 9

Sometimes I'm sure

I'm barren.

Sometimes in the anxious darkness I'm sure

I'm barren.[30]

Today 3:56 PM

At the race track. Love &
Bullies was refusing the
gate. 🩶

30

Sometimes in the get ocean[31] I'm sure

---

31 Can you go to the beach when it's raining, when it's this lush?
  Can we have wet sand?
            There between anything there is
  / and me,
            I'm not sentimental /
  so I feel disloyal /

  so I feel A fawn skeleton / inside this sentence / all sentence
                            cattled / on the shoreline

  I don't believe in awe. I do / A clean hoof lying there / To submit To present
  on A topic /

                            A tension / Not seeing, but SEEING / INSISTING ON /
  A pulse in the mist / A flaw on the lawn / To love what passes by w yourself / To love
  what passes by w out reverence / w another reverence / It matters / that you say / what
  happened to you / I can't stop taking / everything you say IN / IN HERE / AND
  USING IT / TO LIVE / LIVING IT / I FEEL / that's y / I'm raw matter /
                            that's y / I feel disloyal / AND IN LOVE.

110

I'm barren.[32]

---

32 The girl across the table / from me at the reading / with the streak in her hair, / blue or purple or a garden, / insists on gifting me a cigarette / some dark silver / some in-between smelling cloth. I heard you are excessive, she says. Someone said I should talk to you / because you are excessive.

What does it mean when the sentence floats / How to get to it?
What does it mean to speak for the first time in a long time?

Oh, I say, that might be me, / IT IS ME, / but it takes so little / for the world to repeat that I am such / that I am a strange situation of so much.

/ I am a beginning before all that exists / I look at this
word, "excess,"
and think, What turns sour
before it is saved / before it is
space / What is the misery of the diamond? / I am a beginning
in what space is / before it exists. / "The space we love,"
says Gaston Bachelard, "is unwilling to remain permanently
enclosed." "To abolish all signs, and then go after them,"
says Etel Adnan. / My braid comes out of nowhere.

—Dear Alive   / of Mine OR A VOICE / OR A CLOT / OR THE BAY:
WHAT'S IN A GOLD FLECK? WHAT ARCHIVE FACES THE SEA?
WHAT REMAINS INTACT OR LOOKS AWAY IN THE MIDDLE OF
WRITING? ISN'T A NEST AN ANIMAL, TOO?
/ They crouch / They split /

                              Sometimes the New Moon is degrading OR I AM A CROCUS
UNFOLDING UNFLOODING / THE FLOWERBOILS / They crouch / They split
/ the day in half / so that there is no human being, / just the space between the two
/ the two people / the woman and the flower / the woman and the cold islands
/ the person and her pornography / her understanding of contact /

                      / I love / their long redblue strings
                      / I love their redblue strings like they are always resting
                      / after giving birth to the world.

J30

        How is the book an ambient duration? Are you a Leo, too, by chance / by chance im-
agined or real? Bhanu is. So is Ashbery. To keep or not keep / increasing forms. To keep or not to
keep / a smudge, / pleasure and change. It's my birthday, / a coincidence or a vacation, / an interval
in this space, / in this movement of our (N and my) choosing. We're driving around the outskirts of
Savannah, GA. In our choosing, everything that is pained / everything that is painted, / everything
that is J calling me having arrived in California, / is a corresponding text, / deranged or expectant. N
talks to me about the exaggeration of movement / in boy band music videos. Their hands / all detri-
tus and gesture. I think, Shame can't really / kill desire. Or at least not here. To keep or not to keep
/ To strip down partially / In the darkness of a shed. / To be asked then, / While you are being de-
stroyed, / To describe the sky. The ceaseless blur, / It riots. Who will write in, I say to the notebook
I end up keeping / I don't end up keeping. I write about the same sentences anyway, / having looked
away. Effective exposure / deadly following / deadly hairless, / licking. I remember I was watching
the heron lift away, veer, while I was talking or writing. Wonder, encounter. "Dear C," says E in a text,
"I'm sitting outside, looking at a chrysalis and thinking of you. I read in the alphabet book that C is a
camel going beyond itself, / opening itself up to the outside, / crossing Xpanses. C is for cremaster,
/ crumpled foil connecting the chrysalis / to what isn't. I can't look at the chrysalis / and not think
about our hanged woman / her powers. "The Hanged Woman," who is so compelling. "The Hanged
Woman, who shows us, in a collapsing deck, in a cluster, that we achieve genuine independence when
we attach ourselves to the rhythms of the universe, when we dangle and give and herd, when we are
followed haunted fucked and needed." Radiant, shattered marshwater eating the sun's / soft data,
I say to myself when I'm outside of the notebook. Is the surface lit / with sightings / or constant
depth?

112

—I might be *Marie in Gold*
or *Marie in Tar* I might / both be her,

/ a looseness / a HEADSHOT gathered in the cliff / A violet chiffon / A list of everything I've lost.

Dear Alive / of Mine How A Privacy? I might / both be her An emotional silence, / dark seaweed with the sparkling ribbon gone / through it.

How A Woman? / How A Woman / A Privacy? / How A Privacy / If It's Already / So Alien? / If She's Already / An Alien?

/ Marie in Gold or Marie in Tar She is full I might both be her The Long / Withdrawn Thing / It Comes / To Disturb Us.

A1

Dear B, all fur is aimless. Dear B, your name means fiery arrow, I think to myself, while eating dried apricots in the campground. Dear B, I cut you / A SUMMER ROSE / with the people struggling inside. Dear B, it's impossible to convince someone / looking at the surface of the ocean / it's impossible to undertake / the position of convincing / someone looking at the surface of the ocean / that it is dying. It looks so alive. Dear B, it is impossible to write / this letter. To write to you about your blue and splendor and warp / your regeneration. Dear B, Dottie Lasky asked N to answer the question, / What is your favorite color? I dropped flower-shreds in the water. I dropped the lupine flowers in the water. N repeated the question, What is your favorite color, and I replied, Flowers. Dear B, The point at which the ocean is most beautiful to us / is when / it is about to be / forgotten. What did the woman say while talking about the ocean / while trying to talk about its death / so we can think about what it would take / to save it? To make a point / it must feel alive. You must make it out / alive. "I'm not a radical," she said. "I'm not a radical. I'm not a radical. I'm not a radical. I'm not a radical. I'm not a radical. I'm not a radical. I'm not a radical. I'm not a radical. I'm not a radical I'm not a radical. If I'm a radical, / it is because I see what others do / not."

—Atext / my cunning plans.

Atext / my crop top.

Atext / agitates the beloved.

Atext / a list / a fist.

Atext / cultivates / a procession / a growing curve / into what I invent.

Atext / how it runs down your face.

Thezoneoftheimpossible / how it runs down your face.

> Dear Alive of / Mine, The tiredness / of my room / What it means to cut
> / a rectangle into the Earth / To then look up from it.
> / The tiredness / of my room / The grave language of bodies.
> / Is there art / in my memory?
> / Will the theoretical distance between / Fuck Off?
> / I wish / for different words / for a girl / for a temple lip
> / that wants / to be a crawlspace / kissing, / rumbling.
> / I wish for different words
> / because I don't / want to be called anything.

> Dear Alive of / Mine, The danger of trauma, / I said in a letter to S,
> even in its slightest forms, / even in tiny, relentless harm,
> / is how quickly space / for reflection, / for word after word
> translation, / for remarkable trips through, / a whole bunch of
> people lying / down / and looking up at the ceiling, / disappears.
> How little strength there is in reaction, / how little accumulation.
> With only exteriority / against any trembling, / identification,
> / the losing and seeing of one's self in an unlimited number of
> others, / depletes.

A2 – A4

Her sails were covered in Jasmine. Perfume. You could smell her (Cleopatra) coming, I say to M and L on a wet, wilting balcony in DC. Later, in her kitchen in Northhampton, MA, K tells N and me about the floral arrangements Emily Dickinson used to write poems for / the blossoming with the word stuck inside / the gifts she would have sent to her friends. / The pungency of lingering just outside, I say to myself, while stirring soup. Intricate ships, says N in response, quoting Alice Notley. It took us 2-3 Uber drivers to get here / to this place where the balcony is / to this place where the balcony is coming out of the earth. The excess of arrival. Drenched flags. M's Air Jordans. How can you spend money on war? / How can you spend money on art?

Later, climbing out of the third floor of their apartment building and into the rain, I love M and L so much. L and I stand close / and look past the rain / We see glistening pyramids between the water coming down / We see glistening pyramids between the letters in the sky / We see Frida Kahlo in gold and red lying in the desert / in the cracked mud partially propped up on her soft elbow / while plants pour from her soft guts. In my dream the night before, people have gold and red smeared on their foreheads. Blue on their chin. They reach across the counter and give me a pastry. Later, N is reading Kate Zambreno's *Heroines*, and we're talking about re-iteration in the book, / about re-iteration of the book / how A[33] power / how A[34] female power must repeat A[35] thing / so intensely / in order to be heard / in order to be regarded. The excess of arrival / The amount of territory / we have to / express hunger / A[36] power / A[37] female power dying while trying to speak / while trying to say, / You might have seen me / You might have witnessed / me. Scent / and blossom, / Scent and Red Feathers, / they squeal. Mermaids are never going to dream, it says in my notebook. K tells us about the rabbit squeal / THE RED FEATHERS A RABBIT EMITS / just before it dies / RED FEATHERS WHY DO THEY EMIT FROM THE SMALL BODY / just before it dies? It squeals, / not for itself, / not in effort for itself, / but for the potential nearness / but for the potential nearness of another underprivileged creature / in rabbit fur / hidden close by / or underneath / or in the slippage between bodies / between *Marie in Gold* and *Marie in Tar* / between the fear of who you might have to become to create living. "Wouldn't it be amazing if we did something helpful as we died?" says K. L and I stand on the roof, talking / not talking. We face the rain coming down / We face the dark / the sensing moving past us, / We face the pyramids lodged between the water coming down, / We face the pyramids lodged between the letters, / a gathering of sound. Every writer creates his precursors, it says in my notebook. It's a Borges quote I transcribed incorrectly. It should say, "Every writer creates his own precursors." But I don't / own my preceding / I don't collaborate with murderers / I don't own the letters I write to you / but I do know something about being flooded with interconnectivity, about sensing your movements from far away / their vibrating all touching and tension. When I am near to you again / I see that sensing release itself / A[38] pollen / into the air / I know how to soften violence / I begin the hung over day with A in the kitchen by putting coconut milk in my coffee / Close by, N sits on a balcony over Brooklyn. An excess of arrival is an excess of beginning and an excess of risk / A[39] swarm. M doesn't mean to hurt my feelings when he feels he has to explain or translate, in an email, the "way C talks" / the "interesting way C talks." We don't know how to say war is too expensive. We know how to say art is too expensive. Sometimes

33	the pyramids between
34	the pyramids between
35	the pyramids between
36	the pyramids between
37	the pyramids between
38	the pyramids between
39	the pyramids between / intricate ships they change the waters / place around them.

sensing the line / the space between poetry and anything else / is so painful / is so full of inter-connectivity / is so full of mystery going / unrecognized / untouched / and unacknowledged, that I want to swallow a butterfly / I want to swallow the orange segments of the butterfly / THE RED FEATHERS OF THE BUTTERFLY / dying on the clean lawn. We have food in the morning in Brooklyn. We sit on grass where / the shudder is felt. N and I cry saying goodbye to A / because climbing out of the third floor of her apartment building and into the rain, We love A so much / We love so much. She hands me a leaf. It looks like A Chrysalis. I have been here before. I have to heal myself in the alcove of the dream pumping into itself, / Air. I have to heal myself in language and people that are not used / but made here in me / with me / despite me. The excess of arrival. A slew of ribbons. Intricate ships they change the waters / place around them.

—Dear Alive of / Mine,

This place is haunted.

A5

"I refuse to love anybody,"

says Lucius, says a boy, a semi-autobiographical
character Elizabeth Bishop invented in high school for the purpose
of telling her unfinished stories about her
childhood in Great Village, Nova Scotia / Elizabeth Bishop
invented him for the purpose of telling her great sadness /
her mother being dragged away / her great rejection of
herself. I understand so little of Bishop, really, but I was
there, in the house, with N, and the energy surrounding us
was as dark as it was powerful. "Please don't hurt us,
ghosts," I said to the room that made a loud sound / I said
to the room where the woman named Sandra told us the
dead bodies were laid out, / Arthur's coffin, / a little frosted
cake. "I hate the men who made me hate Bishop," I tell N
at the breakfast table. What I mean is, upholding Bishop
and her odd, intense work as a paragon of tradition, / as a
reason to reject incorporating emerging notions of
language's alive-ness into our study of language, / as a
reason I should reject myself, / is despicable. Why is
Bishop a boy in this story? Why does the boy say this
startling thing so suddenly in the middle of the page? Why
is Bishop a boy who refuses / who is ashamed of love
moving towards and away? Because men are part of what
made Bishop hate herself / hate the notion of anthologies
which featured only women / hate women who loved
women like she did / hate as she drank her curious self
away. I know so little about Bishop, really, but I've read
her / but I've felt her in this house / but I've felt her flawed
on the lawn. / This sour lightning, I told N while we were
fighting, is ripping me apart.

117

—Dear Alive of / Mine,

This place is haunted.

Haunting is an excess / an intangible excess of presence / which resembles the face / which resembles / re-assembles / something facing you / which you cannot yet face back / with your face / alone. Haunting is an excess / of barrenness / of absence which can be felt / which can be something from across the ocean / A gap / which bears down on you. A gap / where barrenness / and excess / or abundance / share something I often call longing. I often refer to / longing. J says to me in letter from California / from the place where he is alone, "I have read half your essay I think it is so smart and I love it, it made me sad, the part of us not talking quite as much, but I assume these things move in waves. I'm sure we'll have another wave soon." A wave / A gap / for longing. A song I will like is attached. How many times has a man gathered up a woman's hair / pulled her hair to the top of her hair / to reveal her neck / in this text? I thought it was twice, but when I was running / by the graveyard / I suddenly remembered the picture N and I took in Nova Scotia / how we stacked books up and placed the camera on top / how we stacked books up and captured ourselves / as Ted Berrgian and Anne Waldman / in Maine / how we stacked books up and captured ourselves / wrote to ourselves last summer in a poem called "Labor Day" / in a poem that is a haunting of Berrigan's and Waldman's poem "Memorial Day" / which is a poem about the death of their friend / which is a poem about the death of Frank O'Hara. N and I wrote to ourselves / we stacked books up and captured ourselves / until we were writing a poem / which is a piece of writing / about understanding what the work of love is / what the work of our love of poetry is / what the exploitation of workers / of workers in art continues to be / what the work of our love for each other is. Haunting is copying / Haunting is copying what doesn't go away A gap / the longing in this pattern / the longing in this repetition / A gap / A potential gate / A more urgent portal covered in roses you must eat with your mouth and sleeve / rubbing. I turn around to face it To face it I turn around to bleed into length into what length is no longer / myself / but an unlawful occurrence / a color / I turn around to bleed into a matrix of glass and stone and water pulled back / water bared / I TURN AROUND TO BLEED INTO AN ARRAY / where there is no memory of more roses than there is everywhere.

—Dear Alive / of Mine, Dear No / Soothing Matter, Dear Crystalline Masses
/ You May Take Any Form, Yesterday, N and I went to the beach

It's cooler now, grayer now, steeper now Sexy and full
                                        of discipline / Outside, the pelicans are

/ like faded, prickly gauze or roses strewn in the gutter
                                        between the air / and the water / and killing

Yesterday, N and I went to the beach / and I read Susan Howe's *My Emily Dickinson*
/ the part where she quotes Emily, in a letter, saying,
        "Nature is a Haunted House—but Art—a House that tries to be Haunted"

This month I am haunted by absence.

Yesterday, N and I went to the beach. My period won't come, is paused, / and I am struck in it
/ Where is my future, I think as we're driving along the coast / along the sea / along the shore
/ a tightened spot /

where bones / shells / notes / are twisted or / left to dry out / I am petulant and
encrusted, / a raving mouth / with some beer in it, / a not pregnant puddle /
of strain and muscle / I kill my body for what I need / to survive /

Alice Notley is crying reading her poem / I am crying writing my poem / in the sand
I am going further in / I am crying / while I am further in / my office and unpaid / and
working anyway / trying to say to my students / that there are death warrants in the air
/ hot pink pages / or abandon.

I cover death warrants with my life words, says Alice.

Dear Alive / of Mine,

Can you and I have perceptions of a body that doesn't exist?

Is it between us?

Is it between us, dilating?

The gallery / OUR WELT HORSE / buckles

/ @ our weight / @ our ruin / fattening

/ @ flowerreeking / the shed carcasses of petals

/ pieces from the neck.

Do I inflict my writing on you

Feral and unable to stop approaching / like a waterfall

Do I beat down on you / like fraying / water does crush

/ down stones / until they are / wet and shining

I could not bear it / if it was how /

I came to care for you.

My writing possesses nothing, not you / It is a record

of ancient matter / a bloated wail.

Answer if you can.

We are driving along the coast / of Nova Scotia / of the Bay of Fundy / towards a small place with five islands / clustered together / towards a future / ?? / near a small place that's called Economy / on the map / in the book / We got lost in the cow pastures behind the cemetery / in the long grasses / In the stillness and alarm of long grasses, / there are some wild raspberries to eat / I am constantly repeating myself / here, flooding back in / as the aftermath / or the dream / or a philosophy of crowding / or a multitude / the permanent operation of an altered normality / my overrun / long grasses or blood / ?? / In the car I think of Tan Lin saying / "Painting and poetry are forms of cultural impatience and the uninhabitable" / The graves, / we watch them repeat themselves / An image of a willow tree spreads / itself down onto / Name after Name / or the primitive lines / of the uninhabitable / I'm reading Tan Lin on the porch / The fisherman's boots I borrowed are propped up / on the railing / I notice the holes in them / Near the graves / there's a sign that says you can't leave fake flowers / because there's no one to keep them from turning into / bleached trash / healshredding in the wilderness / "They punctuate given space with hallucinogenic color because they are in color," / says Tan Lin / I wear the boots down to the water anyway / N and I walk along an inlet towards the Bay / The mud is wet and red and sucking / What is a precursor to radiance / Is it a kind of wrecked stillness / a kindness in a stenched pause / marshiness or the softness of encasement and sucking We are so sticky Our remnants glow with longing / or is it stalled / "For example painting is dead or painting is beautiful because it generates one word after another," / says Tan Lin / N stops to take a picture of a hip bone that's washed up / A few feet away we find the rest of / the fawn skeleton / bleached trash / There are no teeth marks on any of the bones, says N / The fawn / The lamb / repeats itself on the graves / of some young paused bones / that must've gotten sick or drowned / I started my period just before we left / just before we were about to start driving back / home to Florida / We came back from the grocery store / where we fought / and I put my hands on the counter in the pantry and began to cry / Decorative Surfaces / Decisive Frontiers / The rock changes from red to black as you move along the shore / N finds a purple fossil that turns more pink when it dries / We touch the seaweed twisted and eating the rock almost like it is gasping / Our first morning in the house we wake up to a car crashing and twisted into the telephone pole near the window in our room like it is gasping / in the Drenched Fog / I put my hands on the counter in the pantry and began to cry / I don't think the house is evil, / I tell N, / but I do think it is possessed / I think I am possessed / a tremendous pulsation / a decorative surface / a decisive frontier / It is almost unbearable / the electricity in lieu of electricity / the facts and the grid / What becomes real in my body / and how does it get there / ?? / Me and what I know / What I do know is what I fear / My ability to create / Space A reef / The ragged lines of it / I live here in order to learn how to speak / The burden or the refrain or the relief or the pearl or the dead and how it studs the rain / Yr work, / it isn't experimental, says A / No one has ever given me that permission, / I answer / While driving back home, / we pass the five islands again / and all the water is gone / the water is pulled back so far / you can walk across it / across an extreme barrenness / across the uninhabitable / We pull over and walk through the long grass / of a cow pasture / towards the shore / While we walk, my boots are falling apart and I think of Mallarmé saying, "Such is my life, devoid of anecdote" / and I nod along / I live here in order to speak / to tell N that I love him / to cut open the extreme tide / that which flexes and folds / to bear open / the water / the earth / Art The writing / which resembles but never repeats / The writing The greatest loss of life I think / is correspondence / The activity of devotion being held and released / There is so much that must be taken from me / I need you / to have it / Answer me / Answer me / Answer me if you can.

READING AS A WILDFLOWER ACTIVIST / PART 1

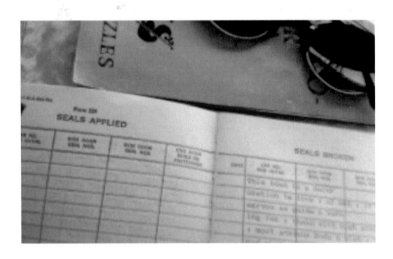

SEALS BROKEN

DATE	CAR NO. AND INITIAL	SIDE DOOR SEAL NOS.	SIDE DOOR SEAL NOS.	END DOOR SEALS OR FASTENINGS
	This book is a decor			
	oration to love : of men : It ever			
	serves as guide & warn			
	ing for : those with high anxiety			
	: most anxious Gods n high : fevering			
	God most anxious God : nice patie			

I begin with photos of Jared Joseph's *The Currant*, an on-going or endless book which translates a Spanish version of the Quran's 6,236 verses into English. It reminds me so much of Edmond Jabès. "Fevering / God most anxious God : nice patio." I, too,[40] have asked J why he writes so much about God when he doesn't believe in God. J is the one who sent me Raúl Zurita while he was in Spain / and I was in Korea. I sent him letters in response, / letters I was wounded on. Pieces of a mountain I'd climbed in Eastern Korea were folded tightly into them. I described seeing, possibly, Japan from the shore. I begin with my friend's book, *The Currant*, on a table in Iowa City, Iowa next to my sunglasses. We're about to walk in the hot air to the graveyard where a statue of a Black Angel is, according to local legend, too dangerous to touch.

Here's Alice Notley on poetry in IC, IA: "So here I am naked for art, / which is a lot of / dumb fucks I already know, / same with poetry. / Written and judged by. Those befoibled guys / —who think—you know / the poetic moment's a pocket in / pool;[41] where can I publish it; what can / I do to my second or third wife now. / Nothing happens in Iowa, so / can I change myself here? Yes" —"As Good As Anything," *Mysteries of Small Houses)*.

J has been publishing pieces of *The Currant* on thrifted grocery lists and automobile inventory sheets. He uses an old typewriter / skills he learned in a bookbinding course offered by the U of I. I begin with a picture of 1 / 1.

---

40 In *Lavish Absence: Recalling and Rereading Edmond Jabès*, our mother of pineapples, Rosemarie Waldrop, who is Jabès English translator, recalls asking Jabès how, as an atheist, he can constantly write of God. He replies that God is a word his culture has given him, "a metaphor for nothingness, the infinite, for silence, death, for all that calls us into question."

41 As I type this excerpt of the poem out, I turn to N and ask if this reference to pool that Notley makes could mean she was hanging out at The Fox Head, a bar J took us to during our visit, a bar that is one of the oldest and most traditional bars in Iowa City / in workshop culture. Much of *The Currant* was written there. $3 for a rail whiskey and a beer back. Ted [Berrigan] would've definitely liked it, N replies. I think of the jukebox and remember watching two fiction writers eat Pop Tarts / drink beer while they shot a game of pool / while young, drunk women threw gummy bears.

Another piece of the text made its way into the 1000 Books / 1000 poets portion of *Poetry will be made by all!*[42] Where is my friend's (unfinished?) book now except everywhere / except every God with / a porch. Where is his book now? Except everywhere you don't expect? Wandering margins / lying on the ground, growing. The book is made of other books / manuscripts / drafts J has sent to me / re-sent to me over e-mail for the past 3? 4? years. *SUP Bulería / Mammal.* Something new shows up in my inbox. *Marilyn.* Never stop growing, says the book. Never stop growing on one surface. Leafing through the 1 / 1, I see fragments of a poem J published at *Claudius App*, on the condition that he changed his name to a woman's name. On the condition that a recording of the poem (to be featured on the site) would be done by a woman. He asked me to do it. Later he made a video, to promote a UK version of *Mammal*, in which he intertwines my recorded reading of the poem with his own. It has the effect of the two of us looking at each other, speaking. How many versions are there? How many versions are there of us looking at each other, speaking? Is it any of it readable? Is any of it a book? How do you NOT get lost in it? In all the possibility the book / our life / possesses.

---

42 1000 books by 1000 poets born in or after 1989* were published by the project *Poetry will be made by all!* Poets were encouraged to submit cobbled together / occasional poems, repurposed text, durational conceptual works that were 100s and 100s of pages long, books that had already been published as books, books that had already been published as online texts, etc. They were encouraged to send the un-publishable, in other words.

*Jared was born the same year I was. 1986. In his bio for the project, he says he was born in 2009.

J goes out to write on the porch every morning N and I are visiting him in Iowa City. J feels further away. We've been exchanging poems for 10 years now, but we don't read each other's work as often anymore. Your manuscript is down there somewhere, he says, when he opens up a white door to show me his room. Maybe it's because we are both working on such long poems / such endless books / such things that simply need to keep moving through writing / that don't need comments or corrections or input so much as they just need to keep moving / to feel that they have permission to do that / to touch the material to create that. Months ago, I sent him what I had written thus far and said, I just need to know you have this. That meant so much to me, he says later on the phone. Do you feel closer to the end, I ask when he returns from the porch in the morning. I'm cooking seitan / some vegetables w / beans + toast soaked in nutritional yeast / vegan butter. N reads us part of a letter from Bernadette Mayer to Bill Berkson. "I'm working on a book about utopias (don't laugh) – this is all your fault, it all began with your question about a good time, which I loved your parody of in the ideal dinner question, it wasn't even a parody. Submissively, your most sincere lounge lizard." It's from a book called *What's Your Idea of a Good Time?* It's a book of questions and answers. Received and sent. The title is based on the first question posed by Berkson. Of course not, J answers.

I don't want to think about the end point or the beginning point of what I work on / of what I read / of our conversation with each other / of our conversation with the earth Art. I want to be continuous in how I register / record. I want to be full of movement concerning How I Feel and Where I Am When I Feel It. I want to be continuous in how I question / in how I answer / in how I receive / in how I send it all to you. I want to be closer / to sensing the process of how it gets written down. I want to be in proximity to the paths, to the decay, to the incisions, the streaks. Who taught me how to get close to my projects? Who showed me how to uncover the bodies? There is an ability to make contact / to follow the mystery of contact, its closeness to me. It comes from site / non-site of the books I keep on a special shelf in the other room. Bhanu Kapil's *Schizophrene*. A book carved into its own species / non-species. A book carved with the bone or the snow. Raúl Zurita's *Song For His Disappeared Love*. A book or a blocked crystal / drifting mirror in the water, the land. Edmond Jabès' *The Book of Margins*. The book / the pieces of it / speaking from an impossible place. These writers / their books offer themselves to me / the writing, and it gets written down in me / on the page as if it were the sea N and I are driving towards.

It is the sea / this kind of reading / this kind of living with / this kind of studying. A leaking extravagance or a chiseling sprawl. Froth and lead. How would you describe it, / the book? I want to think about an image encountered in the world that dominates or could dominate what was previously held up by the writer / by the earth Art. We run from sculpture to sculpture, from forest to forest, drinking coffee. Is that the book? I touch the stones until they touch back / until they begin to smear / until they taste salt in their lungs, too, / from diving so much. Is that the book? The stones, they're alive. When I write about the book or about the books I mentioned here / or above, I want the burning of the forest, the controlled burning of the forest we saw on the way to the beach / to the Gulf of Mexico. A torch made of branches / of flowers made on fire / a bouquet in the writer's imagination growing / scattering / spreading. Is that the book? When you are caught on something / When you are caught on the page / When it catches you / When the expansive-ness of the page catches on to you / up to you / overwhelms you, what is tearing? What rips apart? Do butchers always fall in love with you? Does it hurt / the membranes or the memory? What breaks through? What movement / does it take? How would you have it? How will you meet it? How will you mark it? How will you live through it?

THE BOOK BEGINS / THE BOOK IS LOST: *Schizophrene* — Bhanu Kapil

/ The book is lost before it begins
/ The space of the book is lost
/ The page is lost to movement
/ To the movement of writing
/ To the places where the body is forced
/ To the places where the body is wandering or lost
/ To the places where the body's blood is forced to wander or be lost
/ Through decimated life
/ Its metallurgy
/ Its re-convening
/ Through vibration
/ Through a ghost of the book
/ Held together by a body
/ By a body of work
/ By its movement
/ By the form it
/ Creates
/ Destroys
/ Combines

"Philosophical discourse always gets lost at a certain moment. Perhaps it is nothing but an inexorable way of losing and getting lost. Of this also we are reminded by the degrading murmur: it goes its way."
—Maurice Blanchot

"...*it goes its inky way.*"
—"The Moment After," *The Book of Margins*, Edmond Jabès

Maybe it's not just ink on the page that directs or re-directs the writing or movement of a book / a thing / a writing / in progress. What if there is more texture to it? What if there is more to writing's life and creation? What if it's also clay and stone? Flower and edge? What if it's also water crossing, again / and again, / through several states or countries?

Maybe this is not something the writer can see, but something the writer can feel / lightly touching / her as she moves through page and thought. Maybe it is not something the writer can see, but something the writer can touch lightly / repeatedly / differently / with the word / in an attempt to follow / in an attempt to explore. The writing beyond writing is still writing. The work of the garden is a tangle.

"The upwelling of philosophy attends to what we can't see.
A light tent over the text,"
—"I. Schizophrene," *Schizophrene*, Bhanu Kapil

In the very first pages (an introduction) of her book, Schizophrene, Bhanu Kapil describes standing in the darkness of her garden, her space / the blackness that surrounds her house. She moves her arm, where her book (still in unpublished, notebook form), Schizophrene, is being held. She describes, in this introduction / in these pre-pages, her book vibrating with a potential energy about to become kinetic. Here, her book is about to be released. When she lets go, / her writing is / somewhere else. She decides to make a throwing motion. She decides to make throwing an emotion / She makes throwing an emotion which engulfs / the text as it was / there with her.

"The snow wet the book then froze it like a passive sun. These notes are directed towards the region I wanted to perceive but could not. Notes for the schizophrene night, a schizophrene day, a rapid sketch.

The book before writing, arcing once more through the crisp dark air. And the line the book makes is an axis, a hunk of electromagnetic fur torn into the side of something still living and thrown,

like a wire, threaded, a spark towards the grass."
—"I. Schizophrene," *Schizophrene*

Schizophrene is / the book en route / the book in process. The page is still malleable / still soft / still unprinted / still unprintable. It is unprintable, but written on / but living / but moving anyway.

What happens to the [pre-]text of *Schizophrene*? What happens in the introduction? The reader learns that the finished version he / she holds in his / her hand is not / cannot be the original. The beginning was lost. Each time I read this book, the beginning is lost again. The beginning fails / flails to reveal itself. The ghost of the book begins to flap again. The book began before it arrived in between the front and the back covers / those two lips. The book continues to blossom / in failure / as many.

Before it came to me, / *Schizophrene* had already tried not to die / *Schizophrene* had already tried not to live. And here it is / now / between my hands / both alive and dead. Understanding / seeing the book in this way is to understand / to see that it is so much larger / than any form it takes / in reality. The form it takes in my imagination / is a dripping / blossom. This is actually what language means when it attempts to describe writing as "fluid." The book that pools and spreads. The book that keeps responding to something / a reader can't quite see, but can touch with the color of wondering. The book that keeps responding to something / you know you can feel.

Kapil explains in the introduction to *Schizophrene*, which is entitled "Passive Notes," the consequences of her emergence into and through the darkness of her garden, her space. She explains the consequences of throwing her notebook, her writing, into the weather that causes it to fall apart. She explains the consequences of re-writing the book after this event. She uses italics throughout the explanation to indicate what initial conceptual indicators / what objects and aims / are lost in the rupture of the original text of *Schizophrene* / the sudden movement:

years, to write, epic, trans-generational, schizophrenia, communities; the, domestic violence, disorders, project, felt, the page, surface, deflect, point, pen, the screen, reflective, touch, night, had failed, notebook, draft, house, winter, warm, notes, fragments, the phrases and lines, decayed, pages.

Or rather, she uses italics throughout her explanation to indicate what conceptual indicators / what objects and aims are rearranged in the rupture of the original text of Schizophrene / of the sudden movement. What happened to the unseen / original text of Schizophrene is: the italicized terms are affected. The language is changed / evolved / bloomed. An unexpected potential is found and devoured.

What was completed or almost completed in that "notebook, a hand-written final draft," how those terms were present within that near completion, was re-broken and re-configured by the aftershocks of the on-going event[43] that began the book. The terms of the book were affected by the ground / by the dirt / by the sensations Kapil felt when throwing the book / when picking the book back up / in its newly dead / in its newly alive / form. The terms of the book were affected by something that pushed writing beyond writing. By something I mean, which part of you feels like it is trembling?

---

43 Is there ever an end to Immigration, to the traumatic movement of the body named Immigrant? How does such a movement, stretched and confused / maybe psychotic, says Kapil, affect an Immigrant trying to write? Is this testimony ever acceptable? Does Kapil write anyway? Kapil moves from England to America. She teaches. She writes. She gathers. She goes to India, back to London. She goes to South America. She speaks to other Immigrants. She has been in Colorado since 1998. Her mother joins her and her son. I know this because I read her online diary everyday. I read what she makes constantly public. I lap it up. I cherish it. I think about it when I get up and move. I bring sea glass and sea bone home from the sea. She finds some other way to make the book possible.

The book was lost in the snow. It broke apart and became a corpse there. It became a ghost that haunts the text I hold. A text that is distorted. A text that is throbbing. A text that hears. The book was thrown into a plentiful unknown / into a question / by an eruption / surrounding it / surviving it.

"Social and psychic identifications that disrupt and (re-)envision, to throw into question conventions of codifying

Form as interplay of mobile elements, actuated by the ensemble of movements developed within it

The comportment is one of experiment."
—"Pollen Fossil Record," *Commons*, Myung Mi Kim

/ The comportment
/ The behavior
/ Of beginning to write
/ Is lost to something
/ More complex
/ More audacious
/ More necessary

For Kapil, the behavior of beginning to write the book is lost to the idea that the book couldn't be written. The behavior of beginning to write was lost to the idea that the book had no access to language to begin with. Language had no space for Kapil's body and the stones of her garden wept her a moving water, a moving line on the page that would take her elsewhere, towards a throwing motion. The heart of the Immigrant, the stone on fire, can weep. It can weep and it can burn but it can't die. The beginning of the book emerges from a place that isn't written, that can't be written. It emerges from the ground. It is the heart of the Immigrant, the stone on fire. It is the Florist moving towards or away from the sea. The tides of a body continue after it has washed up onto a strip of land called the shore, called a bone, called the page, called the promise of an expanse, called a texture with a haunting quality, called an edge which releases you to elsewhere, to another intensity of living and feeling through language.

THE BOOK BEGINS / THE BOOK IS LOST: *Song For His Disappeared Love* — Raúl Zurita

"I had once read that when [Raúl] Zurita was arrested[44] the military officers were especially suspicious of a file of poems he had with him, and when I had the chance to meet him in April 2008 he confirmed the story for me. Specifically, the military officers didn't know what to make of the illustrations accompanying the poems. They thought they were secret codes and in response they beat him. Eventually, a senior officer recognized that these were 'garbage,' mere poems, and as he casually tossed the writings overboard, he took from Zurita 'the only thing that told me that I wasn't crazy, that I wasn't living in a nightmare…and when they threw the poems into the sea, then I understood exactly what was happening.'

The pages tossed into the sea were from Zurita's first manuscript, *Purgatorio (Purgatory)*, which he had committed to memory, and which he did not return to until three years after his arrest when he finally felt capable of writing again."
—Translator's Introduction to *Song For His Disappeared Love*, Raúl Zurita Trans. Daniel Borzutsky

---

44 Zurita was arrested in Chile on 9/11/1973, the date of the U.S.-backed military coup led by Augusto Pinochet that overthrew the democratically elected government of Salvador Allende. According to a government commission report that included testimony from more than 30,000 people, Pinochet's government killed at least 3,197 people and tortured about 29,000. Two-thirds of the cases listed in the report happened in 1973. Bodies were disposed of, or disappeared, for the seventeen years of Pincohet's rule using a number of horrific (and almost ritualistic or holy) methods that depended on the vastness of Chile's landscapes. The military code name given to the undertaking was "Operation Television Removal." Bodies (which had been killed and kept or located and dug up / exhumed) or remnants of bodies were thrown from planes into the sea, into rivers, onto mountains. Bodies were dumped into the Atacama Desert, the only desert in the world with zero humidity. It is one of the most ideal places in the world for stargazing. Observatories there contain the most powerful telescopes in the world. "I wish the telescopes didn't just look into the sky, but could also see through the earth so that we could find them," says* one of the many Chilean women who still visits and digs into the Atacama Desert with the hope of unearthing bodies of the Disappeared.

*Quote found in *Nostalgia for Light*, a 2010 documentary by Patricio Guzman.

Purgatory begins with a cut / a laceration / a wound / a gap / a visceral communication:

"my   friends   think
I'm   a sick   woman
because I burned my cheek"

SFHDL begins with a cut / a laceration / a wound / a gap / a visceral communication:

"Now Zurita — he said — now that you got in
here into our nightmares, through pure verse
and guts: can you tell me where my son is?"

A page / Every page of Zurita is every book by Zurita. A page is a small body broken into pieces / into other small bodies that sing to each other / into Men / into Women / into the voices of my small girl / my small boy / that sing to each other from various distances on pages / across pages / in books / between books.

"-   Oh love we burst.
  -        Oh love we burst"
—"11," *SFHDL*

A small body is a small dash beginning the line. A small body is a small dash lying down / or discarded at the beginning of the line. A small body is a small dash disappearing as it is thrown by Zurita's captors from a plane / thrown into the vastness of the Chilean landscape / in an attempt to hide it.

A small body is unearthed by Zurita in the vastness of the page's or the book's landscape. A small body is unearthed through impossible distance, through swerving. A small body, written in the shape of a poem, is an attempt to allow what disappeared, what didn't disappear to re-emerge. A small body is broken, but re-envisioned. A small body is spreading. It is "stuck to the rocks, to the sea and the mountains" —"08," *SFHDL*. A small body of text becomes a perch in the torrent that is Zurita's language and approach to writing.

/ This book is not the one that was lost.
/ It is not the body that was cut,
/ Though it bleeds as it calls or re-calls,
/ As it becomes
/ A CONSTANT R E-C O L L E C T I O N.
/ A CONSTANT WRECK OF COLLECTION.

"AWRECKEDCOGNITION"
—*Poems of a Black Object*, Ronaldo Wilson

/ AWRECKEDCHORUS.

To be lost, you must use all your senses. It's not an act of disorientation. You must watch all your senses bleed onto the lost bodies that are there / that are not there. You must watch all your senses bleed onto the lost pages. All that is lost, all these bodies, still have the ability to make noise, to make sound, to make space necessary for them. What happens to pain and struggle in the lost book / the lost file of Zurita's re-found again and again? Is pain and struggle what permits the lost book / the lost file of Zurita to be re-made? What makes it urgent that the lost book / the lost file be re-formed? Is it another lost body or a piece of a lost body? It is another body touching all bodies that are lost, that were lost. Which part of these poems is dissolution and which parts is careful, powerful re-arrangement, an arrangement previously unseen? Which part simply stands up and dreams? Which part speaks?

"I want stigmata. I do not want the stigmata to disappear. I am attached to my engravings, to the stings in my flesh and my mental parchment. I do not fear that trauma and stigma will form an alliance: the literature in me wants to maintain and reanimate traces.

Traumatism as an opening to the future of the wound is the promise of a text."
—"Preface: On Stigmatatexts by Helene Cixous," *Stigmata: Escaping Texts*, Hélène Cixous

In this book, from the beginning, where blood soaks the body, pain and struggle are collapsed impossibly into love, passion, and promise. "Now the entire universe is you and I minus you and I," "10," *SFHDL*. The writing and voice are collapsed into a complex intelligibility comprised of fragments of the dead and the living, the present and the absent. Every piece touched is accounted for as an intensity, a texture, and a poem. Here are worlds of language moving, getting up, falling / failing. Worlds of language covering the earth, healing it when it is not capable of healing / healing it with bodies and words the book doesn't know / healing it with bodies and words the book has lost / healing it with bodies and words the book knows it has lost.

THE BOOK BEGINS / THE BOOK IS LOST: *The Book of Margins* — Edmond Jabès

A book by Edmond Jabès is assembled by what makes it possible. What makes a book by Jabès possible is the impossibility of God's presence in language / of God's haunting of language. What makes writing possible is a body immersed in that (un)emptiness. The impossibility of God's presence in language / of God's haunting of language / produces a silent, powerful desert Jabès writes and works in. It's a place that destroys the writing and the book as it moves along. Jabès' The Book of Margins exemplifies a necessary deterritorialization[46] of the book as a complete object. The book is replaced by a necessary deterritorialization of language within the consciousness of a(n) (exiled[47]) person attempting to write.

"Deserts of love,"
—"10," *Song For His Disappeared Love*, Raúl Zurita

When language is deterritorialized / When a book is deterritorialized / When Jabès loses the right to occupy the space of Egypt / When Jabès loses God / the word becomes part of an urgency, part of an undoing, an escape,[48] an incalculability. Suddenly the word is given the permission, the space to become a living, visceral entity both separate from / and a part of / the writer.

---

46 Term first encountered in Gilles Deleuze and Félix Guattari's *Kafka: Toward a Minor Literature*.
47 Edmond Jabès was born to a Jewish family and raised in Egypt. When Egypt expelled its Jewish population in 1956, Jabès went to Paris.
48 "All these texts aim to flee the fatal nail, the sword, the knife, the axe which threatens to fix, to nail, to immobilize them in, by, death. Their first and best ally in the evasion is the poetic use of the languages of language. If only we listen, a language always speaks several languages at once, and runs with a single word in opposite directions." —"Preface: On Stigmatatexts by Hélène Cixous," *Stigmata*, Hélène Cixous

In Jabès, the word is given the permission to thrive according to the particular conditions created by the writer's choices, by its proximity to other words, by its proximity to the ghost of other words, by the play and chance the word partakes in given its locations on the page, by the color of the word's dreams, by the earth and noise surrounding the writer at any given moment. The word is given permission to thrive according to the conditions of living / to the conditions of poetry rather than the conditions of craft / literature.

"This language torn from sense, conquering sense, bringing about an active neutralization of sense, no longer finds its value in anything but an accenting of the word, an inflection."
—"What is a Minor Literature?" *Kafka: Toward a Minor Literature*, Gilles Deleuze and Félix Guattari

In *The Book of Margins*, a "sense" of language and a need for it to sustain a notion of order is lost so that a simulation of language (craft) might be avoided. Utilizing language as though it were a simulation of the world does not capture[49] living. It does not transform or even render a life as it moves in and around the words of the page. Thinking of language as a simulation does not enact speaking.

The book and its impossibility are not a copy or a painted landscape of the world, but an ever-growing world[50] within the world. The book is a stone growing wildly / until it becomes a cliff sucked on by the sea. The book is a stone finally given the radical power to speak as a world. A world that spills. A world that oscillates. A world that is charged. A world that startles edges with pressure, fraying them, enumerating them further.

---

49 The use of this word *capture* suggests an important and often unnecessary separation made between the life a writer lives away from the page and the life the writer lives while writing (while writing even when she is not physically writing). The word capture suggests that writing is a (violent) project of wrangling and subduing, of mastery, rather than a project of proceeding exploration, curiosity, and unpredictability.

50 "A successful object, in the sense that it exists outside its own reality, is an object that creates a dualistic relation, a relation that can emerge through diversion, contradiction, destabilization, but which effectively brings the so-called reality of a world and its radical illusion face-to-face." —"First Interview," *The Singular Objects of Architecture*, Jean Baudrillard and Jean Nouvel, translated by Robert Bononno

To write a world is to create an atmosphere. An atmosphere stirs the soil beneath, its gaseous parts have an effect on the soil's richness, but an atmosphere does not predict what will grow or how it will thrive. Here, intense gathering / mixing / collage / conversation occurs until the writer and the words can breathe, can move towards or away from ideas, landscapes, voices, realities, dreams, poetry. If anything is captured, it is the process of writing. To write in this way is / to bloom.

"(Does the book, here, stand for love? The book is an object of love. These manifestations of love in the book are the hugs, the kisses, bites of sentences, words, letters…"
—"The Absoluteness of Death," *The Book of Margins*, Edmond Jabès

A sense of language does not result in a writer's ability to make sense or orders out of language. A structure does not stabilize the book and its language. For Jabès, a structure unleashes the book onto / into the reader, the desert, the air.

Structure is the writer's initiation into painful, necessary accumulation of writings, of letterings. Structure gives the word and its various-ness, its language, a movement, a rhythm. The writer does not construct a book to contain language's vastness. The writer and the book are lost in the possibility of such a thing. The book's structures are constructed in an attempt to suggest that language's vastness is beyond the book it uses to speak. The book embodies a measurement which always changes / which always escapes us. The book is constructed to attend / to listen to a constant hunger felt / to a constant hunger bled or burnt onto the page.

"Black fire on white fire"
—"The Moment After," *The Book of Margins*

In *The Book of Margins*, the book is lost to writing, to poetry, to the impossible intensities of language and a spiritual engagement in its possible processes, which rip apart the book until writing becomes blood on the move, soil filled with lust for growth / flowering.

"To great writers, finished works weigh lighter than those fragments on which they work throughout their lives. For only the more feeble and distracted take an inimitable pleasure in closure, feeling that their lives have thereby been given back to them. For the genius each caesura, and the heavy blows of fate, fall like gentle sleep itself into his workshop labor. Around it he draws a charmed circle of fragments."
—"Standard Clock," *One Way Street and Other Writings*, Walter Benjamin

This book is meant to capture the entire process of losing, of wandering through writing as closely as possible. The book begins, for Jabès, by revealing what makes it, by revealing the difficult exchanges with language that make it. The book begins by revealing all the exchange with other writers (Paul Celan, Maurice Blanchot, Rosemarie Waldrop, Max Jacob, Jacques Derrida, etc.) and books that make it. It begins by creating an exchange between other books (*The Book of Questions*) and characters (Sarah and Yukel) written by Jabès. The book begins by piecing together a correspondence. In the density of correspondence, all writing awaits a question or an answer, a constant point of reception or transmission. In this way, Jabès gives his book the power of a precise, lived continuity.

"It is in this other time, at time's edge, that I find you again, dear Gabriel Bounoure. The infinite suits you. The infinite where your feet carried you and one evening forsook you, and which now alone has the power to name you."
—"Page Without Date, Undateable," *The Book of Margins*

From the beginning, *The Book of Margins* is more interested in the revelation of writing and its traces than it is in the completeness of the book.[51] The book reveals what language cannot do by continuing to live and thrive in language, by continuing to use the word as it morphs in and around the body that reads, the body that writes.

---

51 What erasing goes into the polishing of writing? What fullness might a reader find healing here in this book that is too full / that is overloaded on its relationship to thinking about writing? Jabès almost contradicts his assertions of writing's impossibility. What is impossible still proliferates and embraces the words around it. Another power lives here in both pain and celebration.

THE BOOK DOES NOT END / THE BOOK IS LOST: *Schizophrene* — Bhanu Kapil

"A work beyond recovery"
—"The Unconditional," *The Book of Margins*, Edmond Jabès

"It is psychotic to draw a line between two places.

It is psychotic to go.

It is psychotic to look.

Psychotic to live in a different country forever.

Psychotic to lose something forever.

The compelling conviction that something has been lost is psychotic."
—"7. Partition," *Schizophrene*, Bhanu Kapil

In the Foreword to *The Book of Margins*, Mark C. Taylor includes a small description Jabès wrote of the book. "I would like [the texts gathered here] to be received as writing of the vertigo where book opens to book," Jabès writes. I put *The Book of Margins* on its stomach and open Kapil's book to the section entitled, "6. Vertigo." As I understand it, vertigo is dizziness, an inappropriate conception of your body's movement within an amount of space. What you feel mismatches / causes friction between / what you feel / and what you and others believe your body should be feeling / given its movement. "Vertigo is a symptom of profound attraction. An excess of desire," says Kapil.[52]

Vertigo. When you want so much / you must change / the area / in which your wanting pulsates. When you want so much / from writing / you must change the language / you must change the book.

---

52 "6. Vertigo," *Schizophrene*.

"One day per room. It's raining.

My mother's mother put a hand over my mother's mouth, but my mother saw, peeking between the slats of the cart, row after row of women tied to the border trees. 'Their stomachs were cut out,' said my mother. This story, which really wasn't a story but an image, was repeated to me at many bedtimes of my own childhood.

Sometimes I think it was not an image at all but a way of conveying information."
—"7. Partition," *Schziophrene*, Bhanu Kapil

Vertigo. When your life / its movement / causes friction in the area / causes mismatching in the area / where your movement pulsates. Your movement / your life / pulsates so much / it seems foreign / to those around you. When the narrative skips around / and becomes purple with distance. Vertigo. Racism. Misogyny. They get tangled up in the garden / where the book is tangled up. Vertigo. Racism. Misogyny. India. Fragment. London. Grid. Wet Grid. Pakistan. New Delhi. Fragment. Blockbuster. Queens. The Green World. *Blank-ed out jungle space*. KFC. A graveyard with the man from the bar and his friend. Glass coffin. *Schizophrene*. Athens. Bombay. Shiva Temple. Dreamed up notes. Fragment. Electrobion notes. A swarm adheres to the surface of your city. When your movement / your life / your writing's body / is always too much friction / is always too much rubbing / is always an inappropriate conception of movement / within an amount of space.

When there are ghosts / When there is a writer / When there is a body with so much ambition / to become unbound and unleashed / in questions / in powerful fragments which attempt / which re-attempt to chronicle / to be chronic in their receiving / of where and how the writing and the body don't belong / of the impossibility of the presence of the writing and the body anyway / of how the fragments and the writing and the body feel and speak / as though they belonged to someone / to some space.

When it persists / the ghost of the book / the ghost of a place lost / the ghost in the place gained / the ghost of ancestors / the ghost of others' ancestors in a city, what is the consequence? What if they multiply? What happens when, "All my love is here and it has stayed,"[53] despite attempts to erase it / to call it inappropriate / to call it dizzying? The ghosts, / the fragments of Kapil's lost book, / they broke open the book. / They gather energy / until they can touch each other / until they can touch the reader. They lead the reader into the movement / the color / the mutating intensity of a space. They give the reader a commodious arrival / into the altered space of the book / beyond the book / into the space of feeling while writing / into the space of healing while writing.

"to flux and squat[54] in an inhabited place, risking something"
—"3. Healing Narrative," *Schizophrene*.

---

53 "08," Raúl Zurita, *Song For His Disappeared Love*.
54 "As the girl leans into chiaroscuro, commodiousness* unpleats itself in the interstices of her gestural history and in the time of reading, which becomes a rhythmic infinity. She embodies an unknowable politics by deepening the shadows in places, tarrying with the anarchy of impersonal memory. Her identifications are small revolutions and also the potent failures of revolutions. She is free not to appear."
-"Time in the Codex", *Nilling*, Lisa Robertson.

Robertson's footnote: "The trope of the readerly pilgrimage further complicates itself in the 18th-century secular humanist practice of the Grand Tour, where the journey to Rome can be mirrored, supplemented or substituted by the private perusal of bound print albums such as those of Piranesi. Where the 12th-century reader is on a road towards spiritual light, knowledge of the divine as embodied in the book and the word, the young man on his Grand Tour moves towards shadows, ruins. The self has become not what is lit by divine truth, but what garners an obscurity in the partiality and ambivalence of origins, which are always perceived as lost, broken, in ruin. In Piranesi's albums, the Roman dark etched by the scribbling burin in the new dark of the unconscious, the new divinity."

What is a book but a burst of weeping / or song? A book is a ragged or torn sound and the impossibility of a body / of a writing / to hold such a feeling / such a release.

"I wrote about her body, the vertical grave she created in my mind and in the minds of anyone who heard about her, this anonymous and delicate 'box.' This imprint. This metal animal. This veil of charcoal and vermillion powder, smudged to form a curtain of hair falling over the face. Like an animal almost in flight, but possessed, restricted to the band of earth that precedes the border or follows it, depending on which way you cross; the woman stares, focusing on a point. Someone else is staring too.

Can you smell her burning fur?"
—"3. Healing Narrative," *Schizophrene*

What is a book but a burst of weeping that catches fire? That becomes dangerous in its potency / in its potential. In its potential to do what? To do nothing. To do nothing but touch. To do nothing but become dangerous to the touch. To do nothing but unravel into writing / into poetry / into radical image / eating / swaying / waving. Is it information? Or is it living? Is it living as the Black Angel? The statue too dangerous to touch? It is living as folds? As touching? As touching which could heal, rhythmically? Impossibly?

Schizophrene is a book about a writer who couldn't finish the book because she couldn't exist to write the book. "These electrobion notes, which are not really notes but dreamed up, basic observations which bely the facts, the following fact, which in turn destroys a content as yet unwritten: *I don't exist.*" —"5. Electrobion," *Schizophrene.* Kapil's experience of linguistic violences and exclusion / of spatial violences and exclusion / made approaching the book immediately painful. It made approaching the book an immediate act of dual wounding. "It was a contemporary voice that had the same power as a foundational voice. No." —"8. India, Fragments," *Schizophrene.* When Kapil approached the white space of London / of America / of English / of the page / she ripped it up. She ripped it up by doing nothing / but writing. She ripped it up by letting the book live in nature / by letting the book die in language.

The book is damaged beyond repair / beyond what makes it a book. The book is reversed / returned in a way the Immigrant cannot be / to the place the Immigrant came from / to nothing / to what doesn't exist.

"'Reverse migration...' Is psychotic." —"2. India, Notebooks," *Schizophrene*. Yet the language for such an act exists. The imagination for such an act exists / mutilates Kapil / the living person / until they are an exile / an (infinite) wound in the city / a gaping hole / in the surface / in the map of the city. Writing a book for a reality that doesn't exist in language is psychotic. Finishing a book is psychotic. What movement then occurs? A pulse doesn't finish, it is simply absorbed into the blood it propels. It is a pause / between. A book doesn't finish or become completed, it shows us what can been done through a continuous presence of feeling / sense. Kapil had to complete the book in another way. Kapil had to not complete the book in another way.

"This image knew no bounds."
—"8. India, Fragments," *Schizophrene*

What contains the most "information"? What contains the most "power"? The word? The image? The book? Or is it in the touching / arrangement / of all that is impossibly joined? There is no city. There is a garden where a metal animal writes in pieces / where a covered [by hair, by colored veil, by abandoned forest] girlface writes in pieces. There is no finishing. There is only what emerges from violence / alive. There is only what emerges from violence / dead. There is only what emerges mid-ocean / mid-storm. The pieces destroyed and resurrected in different parts of the body /of the city / of the garden / of the book. The pieces destroyed and resurrected in different parts of the body / writing.

THE BOOK DOES NOT END / THE BOOK IS LOST: *Song For His Disappeared Love*
— Raúl Zurita

"'If you touch it, it's yours,' says the butcher to the housewife as she extends her hand towards the ham. In this way, you are the velvet body of a boy or girl, the raised part of the pattern,"
—"7. Partition," *Schizophrene*, Bhanu Kapil

"This secret)(dream)(is future public tense not remembered never learned,"
—"TWO NOTES ON THE WORLD GOVERNMENT," *Utopia*, Bernadette Mayer

"None of the poetic forms I knew, nothing, could help me…"
—"Preface: Some Words For This Edition," *Purgatory*, Raúl Zurita

Song for His Disappeared Love is a book that speaks The Past as if it were A Future remembered where the poetry of the living and the dead are conjoined / engaged / conversing / touching / weeping for each other.

"The present has miscalculated me,"
—"Face/," *R's Boat*, Lisa Robertson

Song For His Disappeared Love is a book that speaks The Past as if it were A Future remembered where writing a book means speaking / a communal and infinite care for an other's life / a communal and infinite care for an other's death / a communal and infinite care for an other's life in death / a communal and infinite care for an other's life in survival.

"Still I don't know what memory is,"
—"Face/," *R's Boat*, Lisa Robertson

The female body part / the woman's voice / the male body part / the man's voice / the girl's singing / the boy's singing / the girl being dragged / the boy being dragged. Their emergence / their speaking from the bowels of the poem / their speaking with Zurita / through Zurita / at Zurita / them in conversation / in unison / INACHORUS / keeps revealing / reveling / in life / in death / in the waves between / all of them. None of it feels like a memory, so much as something that is happening / an impossible material unraveling / anyway. A book / dug up / and unwrapped by the sun.

"Do you remember, Chilean, when you were first abandoned as a boy?

                                        Yes, he says

Do you remember the second time when you were about twenty?

                                        Yes, he says

Do you know Chilean and pigeon that we are dead?

                                        Yes, he says

Do you remember your first poem?

                                        Yes, he says

                he says yes yes yes yessssoooooooooooooooooo
                ooooooooooooeeeeeeeeeeiiiiiiiiiiiiiii
                iiiiiiiiiiiioooooooooooooooooooooaaaaaaaaaaaaaa
                la   la
                        laa   "

—"22," *SFHDL*

A poetry is / amazing systems that immediately buckle. A poetry is / amazing systems that grow to need more. While many of the poems of *SFHDL* scatter or stretch across the page in multiple shapes, inviting several ways of reading any given poem / inviting various choral readings[55] of any given poem, much of the structure of *SFHDL* emerges and gathers via numerical organization. Every poem is titled by a number, formally even, as poems marked with a single digit number are also accompanied with a 0 (03, 05, etc.) The numerical names of the poems are simply the page number the poems are printed on. Each number / title is much larger than the poem text and located in the far bottom left or right corner of each page instead of at the top of the page preceding the poem text. Every number is grey and watermarked instead of bolded. Instead of lording over the text of the poem, the faded number resembles a recently discarded body disappearing beneath the waves of the sea. Words from the poems themselves also sometimes appear overtop of the title if the structure of a given poem makes its way down to that portion of the page.

---

55 When N taught this book as part of a course at Florida State University, he had six students read various parts of poem #10 at the same time. The multiple ways in which they read their parts, the multiple ways in which their parts began and ended (the various times / the various lengths of sound or noise it took to read), startled the class, he told me. It was also the first time, he said, that they began to understand the book's capabilities.

While the use of numbers could suggest a kind of organization emerging from chaos, Zurita is far more interested in the complex continuity of numbers. The dislocation / dislodging of the title from the top of the page strips away the reverence often afforded to the singular, complete poem. The title / number echoes a pause and a breath in speaking more than it echoes a signal that the poem is about to begin. The use of numbers allows for all the poems of the book to be immediately conjoined, enabling the reader to further sink into structural and linguistic repetitions throughout the poems, and to also see how differently structured formats and linguistic progressions take root and flow into and over each other. Bands of feeling. Bands of text. The numbers allow the poems and their language to become the flexible fascia of a body of work, a fibrous connective tissue spreading throughout the text, linking bloodword, muscleword, and nerveword.

"-All my countries and hometowns call to my love, my beautiful fallen boy.
-They're all here, they float in the niches,"
—"12," *SFHDL*

The use of numbers in this spiritual and particular way re-envisions the mass ordering that occurs in and around horrific events such as Pinochet's coup d'état. A body count is meant to give television watchers and news article readers an immediate estimation and simulation of scale, of tragedy, of horror. However, Zurita's use of numbers doesn't suggest a finite or comforting sense of where the bodies begin dying and where they stop dying, of where a particular community of people suffered and then began recovering. Instead, the progression of numbers and the progression of poems alongside it, suggests an enactment and a hunger that can and will occur again. The numbers in the book stop at 23, but the words present on the page, imply perpetuation and continuance through language and without it. "Yes, he says" —"23," *SFHDL*. No punctuation is given to stop the sentence or the sound of it. "Yes, what is, finally perpetuated?" asks Jabès in *The Book of Margins*. For Zurita, the book and the poem and the yes and the number is a language of continuance and a constant repetition which he and the voices that surround him have all and no power over. What does it mean utter survival? What does it mean to look for how the dead continue to survive? Is that haunting or is that a kind of living despite?

"Could it be that for the writer everything happens in a forebook whose end he cannot see, whose end is in his book? But nothing happens that has not already happened. The book is at the threshold. This also confirms your cherished project, your declared course, whose ambition might strike us as paradoxical since it is a matter both of undermining the road and of continuing it, as if it could exist only in and through these successive continuations,"
—"The Moment After," *The Book of Margins*, Edmond Jabès

To exhaust the event. To exhaust the meaning of the event until each time it is felt. To exhaust the meaning of the event until its limits and possibilities are re-broken. To exhaust the meaning of the event until each time blood pours out of some new body in the landscape of the page / of the book. To exhaust the meaning of the event until it is infinite. To exhaust the meaning of the event until it is vibrating with energy. To exhaust the meaning of the event until it is a circulation of poetry and breath. To become exhausted in your search for a body and a book which could speak the event. To exhaust yourself until you or the event stretch, finally, beyond the word.

THE BOOK DOES NOT END/ THE BOOK IS LOST: *The Book of Margins* — Edmond Jabès

"The typical work of modern scholarship is intended to be read like a catalogue. But when shall we actually write books like catalogues?"
—"Teaching Aid," *One Way Street and Other Writings*, Walter Benjamin

A catalogue is an inventory, a collection of items, an area of where documentation can be held and distributed / dispersed. A catalogue is a place that can always make room for more information, for more items, for re-writing. Poetry is a mouth or a catalogue for the lost, a catalogue for the attentive obsessive lost in a vastness of writing, a catalogue for the enthusiast.[56] A catalogue, a place where a desire may be depicted or even potentially acquired. A catalogue, a place where desire is sure to grow. An un-ending project of desire. A catalogue, a desert.

carrielorig
@carrielorig

A DESERT IS THE FUTURE OF STONES

Reply   Delete   Favorite   ... More

RETWEETS   FAVORITES
2   2

12:54 PM · 7 Jun 2014

---

56 The epigraph for Susan Howe's *The Noncomformist's Memorial* is a quote marked by Herman Melville in his copy of *Shelley Memorials*. "The enthusiast suppresses her tears, crushes her opening thoughts, and—all is changed."

The Book of Margins is an amassing of writing, a constant in-flux. It is a catalogue of propulsion through writing as it progresses, doubles back, changes form, loses track of no place and of God. It is a fascination with knowledge as it breaks apart. "Every impulse of my body is a recorded, counted trace, multiplied by fever—by love, pain, delirium." —"There Is No Trace But in the Desert," *The Book of Margins*, Edmond Jabès. As it resonates, / it breaks into wonder / into awe / into an unanswerable, but follow-able question. WHAT IT IS / TO BE / TRACEABLE. The dying thing and the living thing suck on what is near to it. Here, writing is the perpetual task of tracking what enters into the field of the page, / of perception. The writer's only end is to create an opening into further space / into further alteration / into further velocity or swing. The writer's only end is a glimpse, / an encounter with / "Book of Famine, Book of Attempt, Book of Money, Book of Labor, Book of Utterance, Book of Hollow Organs, Book of Tending, Book of Wars, Book of Household, Book of Protection, Book of Grief, Book as Inquiry" —"Pollen Fossil Record," *Commons*, Myung Mi Kim.

carrielorig
@carrielorig

I'M WRITING A PAPER ABOUT ALL THAT
PRECEDES ME

↶ Reply   🗑 Delete   ★ Favorite   ••• More

FAVORITES
2   🖼 🖼

10:01 AM - 7 Jun 2014

Jabès makes common what feels remote: the power of writing. The power of writing to sensate in the secret[57] light / and density of the attentive human body as it gets close to it / as the forearm touches the page / as the forearm carves into the page. To give form to what is remote. To give form to all that precedes you. To give form to that kind of distance. To rehearse the book as it deteriorates into the bleeding / that is all that precedes you / that is the distance apparent in the river that flows away from you / or through you. "Any trajectory is dense / outside the threshold / Turn again and lean against / Moving away into depths / of the sea," —"Immediate Acts," *The Noncomformist's Memorial*, Susan Howe. To give form to what is remote for the fear / the love of wandering, for the fear / the love of work. To watch the flowering tree / as it exceeds / its form.

"He was afraid of the black of ink; this was why he wrote.

Most writers, nowadays, are not afraid of anything."
—"On Fear, I," *The Book of Margins*

Rather than reading *The Book of Margins*, / I save pieces of it / almost without knowledge / without trying. I save pieces of the book with pieces of other books. Is this what Jabès means by where book opens to book? I read or write until they are together. I force them together. I wash them in each other. I lick the pages and press them to different parts of my body. I overthrow the question of my body. I lie down. I lie down on the ground and watch the pages flutter, try to get up. How will they work on me?

"Poetry, the permanent mystery into which all mysteries enter."
—"The Man with the Secret (*Max Jacob*)," *The Book of Margins*

---

57 "The man with the secret, not with the legend."
—"The Man with the Secret," *The Book of Margins*

The book does not end by completeness, but by proximity. Mystery is not closeness, but the possibility of closeness. How will it arrive? Mystery is motion's future. What changed motion will inevitably touch me?

"What ties one writer to another lies beyond praise, in the most intimate and most silent part of their being. That is the site of their closeness, at the heart of an adventure that annuls their differences."
—"Extract from a Speech," *The Book of Margins*

My relationship to literature, I came to it through reading. Through feeling words enter into the permeable portions of my body's knowledge. Through entrances I could not predict or find myself. E sends me an email with a quote from Bernadette Mayer. "Thought of yr paper (What is / what should we call this thing?)," it says in the body / of the email.

"What lean in all directions? Chimneys appear to
move. the cake is breathing. to be breathing cake. to be breathing dolphin to be
breathing investments to be breathing prisoners to be breathing all prisoners
chimneys appear to move. many on the mountain may make it fall,"
—*Moving*, Bernadette Mayer

Or did I come to my relationship to literature, to my understanding of how it would both dec-imate and expand my life (I am the book, I say. I repeat this to myself and understand. I look back to the page in the book and see that's not exactly what Jabes says.) through writing? The first writing was only tracing over the letters of books I was learning to read. I traced the whole of them. I pretended the books were my own. Then, I began to change the ends, to work on them. I began to practice alteration until I began to see what it could do for color, for excess, for buried champagne bottles, for rituals of grief, for rituals of nature like thunder, for melted butter rubbing against and also sliding off, for the tiny animal bones that wash up on the beach, for inversion, for layers, for tenderness, for my ability to love others, for my ability to combine the energies of reading and writing.

N and I are in the car, driving towards the sea, driving towards the sea with food. No, that hasn't happened yet. I am writing a future I know. I am writing a future I need to transform. I am wearing a kind of cloth I will take with me into the water. What I understand, I say to N with my arm moving gently in the wind outside the car, is that I will never write a book. The freedom of a forest fire or the knowledge of a flower.

"I don't know. I know we have to find a way to move through the garden,"
—"June 3, 2014," Bhanu Kapil

The book does not end by completeness, but by proximity. The book does not end. It grows. It grows wildly or softly through our ability to bring ourselves to writing / to writing a book. It grows through our willingness to risk closeness.

READING AS A WILDFLOWER ACTIVIST / PART 2

I think about the terrible space between sentences.
I think about the terrible space between sentences.
I think about the terrible space between sentences.
I think about the terrible space between sentences.
I think about the terrible space between sentences.
I think about the terrible space between sentences.
I think about the terrible space between sentences.
I think about the terrible space between sentences.
I think about the terrible space between sentences.
I think about the terrible space between sentences.
I think about the terrible space between sentences.
I think about the terrible space between sentences.
I think about the terrible space between sentences.
I think about the terrible space between sentences.
I think about the terrible space between sentences.
I think about the terrible space between sentences.
I think about the terrible space between sentences.
I think about the terrible space between sentences.
I think about the terrible space between sentences.
I think about the terrible space between sentences.
I think about the terrible space between sentences.
I think about the terrible space between sentences.
I think about the terrible space between sentences.

I think about the terrible space between sentence Dear Alive / of

Mine,

What word have I used yet?

What word have I used yet? I think to myself lying in my bed / recovering from another nightmare / about adjuncting / that the teenagers smoke on top of.

Dehiscence, I write in / between classes in / between the margins of Fred Moten's "Blackness and Nothingness (Mysticism in the Flesh)," is a previously closed piece of
 skin /

a previously closed indwelling of blood / shedding / or about to dream / Your skin scared and free /

You yourself, A Beginner /

reopening / as An Impact

/ or Flowers at the Spine

/ having a nightmare

/ the teenagers smoke on top of.

In the margins in between classes I write, / A Flower is / A Fruit and A Wound.

A Flower is / A Fruit and A Wound,

is what I think when a Man tells me

a Man who heard me read / said,

"I wish she wrote the way she talks."

I recognize a Man is repeating a Man

in order to tell me something about

my work / is unrecognizable

/ uncomfortable / unquotable /

I did not come to poetry in order

to talk / I came

to speak /

to accept the labor of speaking,

exhaustion,

my adjunct hours /

to interarticulate

THE FALLS, THE FALLS.

I feel a draft of Red, a ripping between the language, I say, lying in the bed with my eyes closed. I came to poetry in order / to write. I came / because the shapes and behaviors of the earth are bursting / are how it ends / with you.

I misread a part of the interview where Lauren Berlant says to Claudia Rankine, "I think we see the same thing." What I see when I read is / I think we are the same Thing, / a churning. Reading / it is weirdly like hearing myself, I misread for the second time / further down the page.

The underlined lines in English are: "THE CONCLUSION IS GROWING," and "THERE IS A KIND OF UNDETERMINED HAIR" and "SHE—SHE HER CREDENTIALS"

I think about the terrible space between sentences / between my classes and the cliff / the cliff where the water meets my fragment. It takes forever to know / and even then you are surprised / and even then there is the unbearable / the unquotable encounter / and even then you receive the delayed gifts splitting the roses in the sunset like rotted cram / like rotted cream and even then you say, "The grooves of disruption in your back / the Flowers at the Spine, / traversed."

What happens when I stand close to you? What happens when I stand or speak between my classes and the cliff / the cliff where the water meets my fragment? I am going to fail, fail, fail / each other. My writing / unreliable. My writing / unpredictable. My writing / as relentless or as useless / as thought / as a headdress / a sharp engulfment collapsing into a stream / the doors open to the rain.

E writes me an email re: Gertrude Stein: "Read COMPOSITION AS EXPLANATION today with my class. And it was unsettling to compare our epoch with Stein's—she had faith in equilibrium and centers and it seems our faith needs to acknowledge failure and the amplitude in its wake. Faith is a weird word, but I think it fits. It fits and I love you."

You write back to me, anyway

Anyway, you write back to me

quickly / in the middle

of the night,

"You have changed.

You are much changed.

Your syntax changed,"

you say.

ACKNOWLEDGEMENTS

I would like to thank the following editors (and layout gods) / magazines for publishing pieces from this book: Steven Karl and Dan Magers @ Sink Review, Mark Cugini and Laura Spencer @ Big Lucks, Nate Slawson @ The New Megaphone, Jordan Stempleman @ Continental Review, Stephen Danos and Dolly Lemeke @ Pinwheel, Kimberly Ann Southwick and Sophie Klahr @ Gigantic Sequins, Kelin Loe and Leora Fridman @ Spoke Too Soon, Adam Fell @ Verse Wisconsin, Brandon Shimoda @ ANCIENTS (the stack), Natalie Eilbert @ The Atlas Review, Nate Pritts @ H_NGM_N Books.

I would like to thank the Elizabeth Bishop Society in Great Village for opening up Bishop's childhood home to writers for brief residencies. Our time there yielded growth written / unwritten.

There are so many people I love and need / There would be no reason for language without you. Thank You My Friends / My Family:

Nick Sturm Uttering Light of My Life I Love You, Elisabeth Workman and Bridget Mendel The Three Goddesses With Their Three Cups The High Priestesses Who Taught Me How To Wear A Headdress I Love You I Love You Wednesday Beer Tops, Peter Jurmu My Undying Editor The Gentlest Fighter Who Asked Me If I Had a Book At a Dance Party in Boston, Jared Harvey Who Has Always Been The Most Important Desert Inside Me, My Parents and Sister Who First Gave Me Love, Kelin Loe and Leora Fridman My Curly Wilderness Family My Energy Beacons, Alexis Pope and Caroline Crew Who Suffer And Live Who Suffer and Flourish Who Power Me, Michael Krutel and Jamie Suvak The Quiet Importance Of Being In A Space With You, Cassandra Troyan A Conversation That Birthed My Title The Woman Velvets Darkness, Mark Cugini My God My God Yr Heart, Laura Spencer Who Always Teaches Me About Rioting / Quietness / Roof Standing, My Wonderful Impossible Poetry Students Who Helped Me Complete This Book By Trusting Me With Their Reading, Mary / Feng Sun Chen The World's Important / Depthless Coral Reef, Layne Ransom Who Bleeds Who Bleeds With Joy, Amelia Foster Who Is The Most Patient Loving Person I Have Ever Lived With, Mike Rowe Who Wrote Me Email Who Has Always Helped Me Feel Known / Illuminated Despite Our Struggle, Sally Franson Total Blossom, Natalie Eilbert Swan Explosion, Christie Taylor A Snowstorm A Gorgeousness, Gale Marie Thompson Who Sent Me Singing in the Dark Who Let Me Write Her A Letter, Brandon Shimoda Who Wrote Me A Letter, Sara Woods Who Is My Root / My Stone, Maria Damon Stuart McLean and Leslie Morris Who Fought For My Work / Our Intellectuality / Our Poetics, Austin Hayden My Little Brother

My Walking Friend, Ashley Ford Strong Faith Inspiration, Claire Donato Blue Window, Jordan Stempleman Music Man, Mike Young Who I Feel Has Always Seen Me Quietly / Powerfully, Steven Karl Dark Eclipse Dancer in the Parking Lot on Fire, Jennifer Fossenbell Isabel Harding Anna Rassmussen Zoe Miller Nasir Skandaar Katherine Lee Julia Marley Elizabeth O' Brien Elena Carter Alexandra Watson Laura Scroggs Aaron Apps Lucas De Lima Chrissy Friedlander Kristen Fitzsimmons Florencia Lauria Victoria Blanco and Scott Parker My Cohort in Excess Who I Love and Love, Who I Love and Love and Love and Thank and This Gratitude and These Flowers Which Are Ours.

Special thank you to Bhanu Kapil, Edmond Jabès, Lisa Robertson, Alice Notley, Bernadette Mayer, Etel Adnan, Myung Mi Kim, Raúl Zurita, and to what I could not know / how to live without.